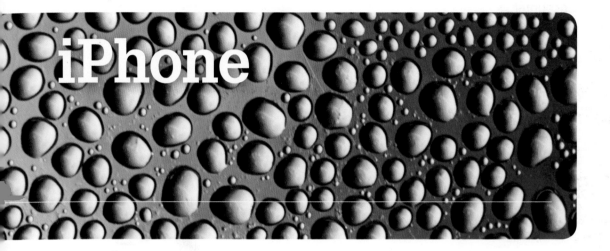

iPhone

in **Simple** steps

Joli Ballew

Use your iPhone with confidence

Get to grips with practical tasks on your iPhone with minimal time, fuss and bother.

In Simple Steps guides guarantee immediate results. They tell you everything you need to know on a specific application; from the most essential tasks to master, to every activity you'll want to accomplish, through to solving the most common problems you'll encounter.

Helpful features

To build your confidence and help you to get the most out of your iPhone, practical hints, tips and shortcuts feature on every page:

! ALERT: Explains and provides practical solutions to the most commonly encountered problems

HOT TIP: Time and effort saving shortcuts

▶ SEE ALSO: Points you to other related tasks and information

? DID YOU KNOW? Additional features to explore

WHAT DOES THIS MEAN?
Jargon and technical terms explained in plain English

Practical. Simple. Fast.

in Simple
steps

Dedication:

For Allison, what an enchanting time to come into the world!

Author acknowledgements:

I'd like to thank Steve Temblett, Robert Cottee, Natasha Whelan and the rest of the gang at Pearson Education for selecting me to write yet another In Simple Steps text. I've lost count, but I think we're closing in on a dozen titles together. Thank *you* for purchasing this text too, and for placing your trust in me to teach you how to use your new iPhone. You can take what you learn here about apps, navigation and iCloud and apply it to future versions of the iPhone, as well as iPads, iPods and other iDevices. The knowledge you gain here will go a long way.

I would also like to thank my agent, Neil Salkind, PhD, from the Salkind Literary Agency. We've been together for a decade, and during that time we've managed to publish 40+ books together. Over the years, we've become friends too. And finally, I'd like to acknowledge my family, including my dad, my daughter Jennifer, her husband Andrew and my partner Cosmo. They are very supportive of me and of my work and I appreciate and love them dearly.

Publisher's acknowledgements:

The publishers are grateful to the following for permission to reproduce copyright material:

Google.Inc for screenshots in Chapter 4 © Google 2012 and YouTube screenshots in Chapter 10; Amazon.com,Inc for screenshots in Chapter 6 © 2012 Amazon.com,Inc and its affiliates, all rights reserved.

In some instances we have been unable to trace the owners of copyright material and we would appreciate any information that would enable us to do so.

in **Simple**
steps

Contents at a glance

Top 10 iPhone Problems Solved

Contents

2 Learn iPhone basics

3 Meet Siri

8 Use the camera, take video and explore FaceTime

9 Stay in touch and be organised

Top 10 iPhone Problems Solved

Top 10 iPhone Tips

Tip 1: Connect to a Wi-Fi network

When you want to connect to the Internet, your iPhone first attempts to connect through a free Wi-Fi network. If it can't find one, it will use your cellular data network. Because you have to pay for the latter, and because you likely have a limited data plan, it's in your best interest to connect to Wi-Fi networks whenever they are available.

1 Get within range of a known Wi-Fi network, such as one at your home, or at a local library, pub, cafe or hotel.

2 If you are prompted to join the network, tap Join.

3 If required to type a password, do so.

4 If you are not prompted to join a known Wi-Fi network:
  - Tap Settings.
  - Tap any required 'back' buttons to return to the main Settings screen.
  - Tap Wi-Fi (it will show Not Connected).

···· AT&T LTE	10:49 AM	▭
Settings		
✈ **Airplane Mode**		OFF
🛜 **Wi-Fi**	Not Connected	>
✳ **Bluetooth**	Off	>

? DID YOU KNOW?
Wi-Fi networks are almost always noticeably faster than cellular networks.

⚠ ALERT: Wi-Fi must be enabled to connect to networks. If applicable, turn Airplane Mode off and Wi-Fi on.

- Tap the desired network to connect to.
- Type a password if applicable.

5 By default, Ask to Join Networks is turned off. Turn on if desired.

..ıl... AT&T LTE	9:19 AM	

| **Settings** | **Wi-Fi** | |

| **Wi-Fi** | | **ON** |

Choose a Network... ⟳

Home	🔒 ≈ ❯
OZOP4	🔒 ≈ ❯
VG6UB	🔒 ≈ ❯
ZEZ83	🔒 ≈ ❯
Other...	❯

| **Ask to Join Networks** | **OFF** |

Known networks will be joined automatically. If no known networks are available, you will have to manually select a network.

HOT TIP: When you want to download apps, movies and media, make sure you're connected to Wi-Fi; otherwise you'll use up your monthly data quota quickly.

Tip 2: Take a photo

The camera icon is on the Home Screen of your iPhone. You tap it to open the camera and take pictures. The camera screen has several features; to take a basic photo you simply select the front- or rear-facing still camera and tap the shutter icon.

1 Auto – Tap to turn on or off the flash. Leave this to its Auto setting to let your iPhone decide what is best for each shot.

2 Options – To turn on the grid and/or HDR (high dynamic range), or take a panoramic picture. HDR offers a higher quality picture that results in varying levels of improvement depending on the shot, but takes longer and more space to save.

3 Switch lenses – To switch from the front- to rear-facing lenses and back again.

4 Thumbnail – To see the last picture taken (and to open the Photos app).

5 Shutter – To take a picture.

6 Camera mode – To switch from the still camera to the video camera.

HOT TIP: To take a video instead of a still picture, move the slider on the bottom right to the video camera, and use the shutter button to start and then stop recording.

? DID YOU KNOW?
You can tap the screen once to let the iPhone focus.

Tip 3: Have Siri look something up on the web

If you only have one hand free and you need to find something on the web quickly, you can ask Siri to look it up for you.

 1 Press and hold the Home button.

2 When you see *What can I help you with?*, say, 'Siri, how do I tie a sailor knot'. The microphone must be purple for Siri to hear you.

3 Note the results. If desired, tap any result in the list to go to the web page.

What can I help you with?   i

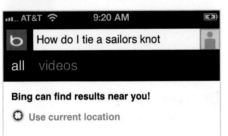

.ıl.. AT&T 🛜   9:20 AM

b How do I tie a sailors knot

all videos

Bing can find results near you!

⊙ Use current location

How to Make a Sailor Knot |
eHow.com
The sailor's knot, also known as the anchor
knot, is one of the easiest knots to tie. It's also
very stable. The sailor's knot was originally
designed to tether up a...
www.ehow.com/how_5175073_make-sailor-
knot.html

How to Tie a Sailor's Necktie |
eHow.com
How to Tie Sailor Knots. A sailor's knot,
otherwise referred to as an anchor knot or
carrick knot, was originally devised to tether
two ropes together.
www.ehow.com/how_5879675_tie-sailor_s-
necktie.html

🔥 **HOT TIP:** If you leave the *What can I help you with?* window open too long without saying anything, it will become inactive. You'll have to tap the microphone icon to make it active so you can talk to Siri when this happens.

🔥 **HOT TIP:** If you aren't comfortable talking to Siri, do your best to overcome it. When you do things without typing, you do them faster and save wear and tear on your hands, fingers and wrists.

🔥 **HOT TIP:** If what you say and what Siri searches and provides results for differ, tap and hold the mouse to correct the text, or just ask Siri again.

Tip 4: Add a photo to an email

You can attach a photo to an email in progress. Just double-tap inside the body of the message, tap the right arrow, and tap Insert Photo or Video. However, you can select up to five photos at once from the Photos app and opt to share them via email instead. Sometimes, this is more convenient.

1 From the Home screen, tap Photos.

2 Tap any 'back' buttons as required to get to the Photos landing page. Make sure Albums is selected.

1:42 PM · AT&T

Albums   Edit

Camera Roll (348) >

Photo Library (860) >

Allison Favorites (22) >

Friends (31) >

Houses (298) >

Me, Jennifer, Mom,... (190) >

My Favorites (60) >

Pets (144) >

Albums   Photo Stream   Places

SEE ALSO: The section Explore the Photos app, in Chapter 7.

HOT TIP: Landing pages for apps don't have a 'back' button.

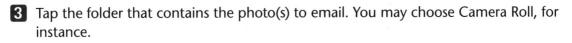

3 Tap the folder that contains the photo(s) to email. You may choose Camera Roll, for instance.

4 Tap Edit, and then tap up to five photos to email.

5 Tap Share.

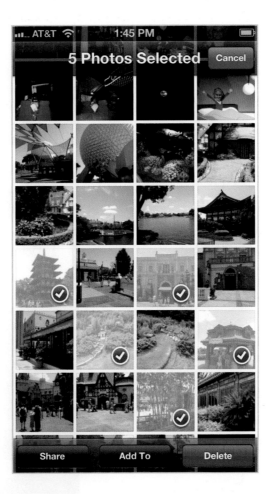

6 Tap Mail, and choose a photo size.

7 Complete the email as desired; tap Send.

> **HOT TIP:** When emailing photos when you aren't connected to Wi-Fi, choose a smaller photo size when sending. If you're connected to Wi-Fi you can choose a larger size without having to worry about your data limits.

Tip 5: Set a reminder with Siri

A reminder is an element of a to-do list. Once reminders are set, upcoming reminders are available from the Reminders app and the Notification pull-down list. The easiest way to set a reminder is to ask Siri to do it.

1 Tap and hold the Home button.

2 When the microphone icon turns purple say 'Remind me'. If is not purple, tap it.

3 Answer Siri's questions. You can say something like, 'I have a meeting tomorrow'.

4 Continue to answer Siri's questions, and when prompted, say 'Yes' to confirm.

5 Note the reminder (do not check it off here). Tap the Home screen to close Siri.

? DID YOU KNOW?
You can view your reminders and mark when you complete them from the Reminders app. For more information, refer to Chapter 9.

! ALERT: You must be able to access the Internet to use Siri. You must also have enabled Siri in Settings > General > Siri.

▶ SEE ALSO: Learn everything you ever wanted to know about Siri in Chapter 3.

Tip 6: Understand iCloud

iCloud is a virtual and physical place on the Internet where you can store data. Apple provides 5 GB of iCloud space for you to use, for free. When you store data in iCloud, you can access all of it from other iDevices, and some of it (Mail, Contacts, Calendars and so on) from almost any Internet-connected computer, tablet or laptop.

- iCloud has its own tab in Settings.

Settings

General	>
Sounds	>
Brightness & Wallpaper	>
Privacy	>
iCloud	>
Mail, Contacts, Calendars	>

- iCloud offers an easy way to back up important data, such as contacts, notes, bookmarks and photos you take with the iPhone's camera.

- You can opt out of iCloud if you like, or only store specific data there.

HOT TIP: Set up Find My iPhone as soon as possible. This will help you find your phone should it go missing, provided it is turned on.

DID YOU KNOW?
Purchases you make from Apple, either from the iTunes store or the App Store, are stored in iCloud for free, and do not count towards or against your free 5 GB limit for data storage.

- When you use iCloud with multiple iDevices, changes you save to iCloud can be synced to other devices easily. If you make a change to a contact on your iPhone, for instance, that change can be sent to your iPad automatically.

- Some data you store in iCloud can be accessed from any computer that is connected to the Internet at www.icloud.com.

 **HOT TIP:** Use your Apple ID for all iCloud use.

Tip 7: Set up Home Sharing

If you have a wireless home network and your iPhone can connect to it, and if you have media to share, you can enable Home Sharing. Once enabled on both your computer (via iTunes) and your iPhone (via Settings), you can share media between them. This means, for one thing, that you can access media stored on home computer(s) from your iPhone without actually having to place the media on it.

1 At your computer, open iTunes. The computer should have media you want to share saved to it. Then, in iTunes:

- Click Advanced.
- Click Turn on Home Sharing.
- Follow the prompts to enable this feature.

2 From your iPhone:

- Tap Settings from the Home screen.
- Tap Music or Videos (either will work).
- Under Home Sharing, type the Apple ID and password you used to configure Home Sharing on your computer in step 1.
- Tap Done.

••• AT&T 🛜	3:59 PM ⬛
‹ Settings	**Videos**

Start Playing   Where Left Off ›

Closed Captioning   (OFF

Home Sharing

Apple ID: joliballew@gmail.com

! ALERT: You can only access shared network media when your iPhone is connected to the home network and the computer that contains the media is turned on and awake.

🔥 HOT TIP: If you're really into listening to music on your iPhone, consider iTunes Match. For a yearly fee, you will have access to your music from virtually anywhere.

Tip 8: Hold a FaceTime conversation

There are two ways to start a FaceTime conversation: either from a Contact card or while in a voice call with a FaceTime contact.

 1 From a Contact card:
- Tap FaceTime.
- Wait for the recipient to answer.

2 While inside a voice call:
- Tap FaceTime.
- Wait for the recipient to accept.

3 To end a FaceTime call, tap End.

.... AT&T 📶 10:10 AM 🔋

Mary Anne Cosmo
00:01

| 🎤 mute | ⚏ keypad | 🔊 speaker |
| add call | FaceTime | contacts |

📞 End

? DID YOU KNOW?
You can hold FaceTime conversations with owners of compatible iPads too.

🔥 HOT TIP: You call tell Siri to initiate a FaceTime video call. Just say, 'Siri, FaceTime <and then state the contact name>'.

Tip 9: Get a free app

One of the tabs in the App Store is Charts. This is a great place to get your first app because you know the apps listed here are popular, and one of the available options is Top Free.

1 Tap App Store on the Home screen.

2 Tap the Charts tab at the bottom of the screen.

3 Scroll through the free options.

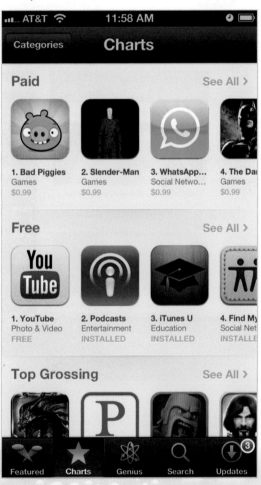

WHAT DOES THIS MEAN?

App: A small program that enables you to do something. You can keep track of the calories you eat in a day, play a game, post a picture to Facebook, subscribe to a music service, and even download a web browser to replace Safari.

4 Tap any app you find interesting.

5 If you decide you want an app, tap Free, then Install App, type your password and tap OK.

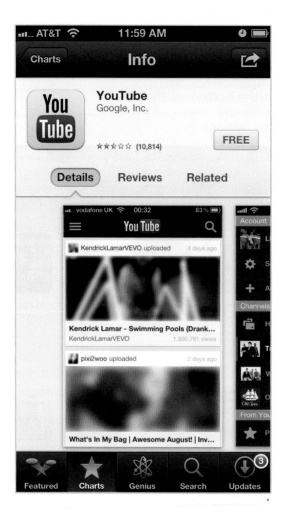

! ALERT: What you see in the Charts list changes often; what you see won't match what's shown here.

Tip 10: Enable Find My iPhone

If you enable Find My iPhone, then, if your iPhone is ever lost or stolen, and it is turned on, you can find out where it is from any computer or compatible Internet-connected device. You can also send a message, erase the data, and more, all from a remote location.

1 Tap Settings, then iCloud.

2 Next to Find My iPhone, move the slider from Off to On.

3 Tap Allow.

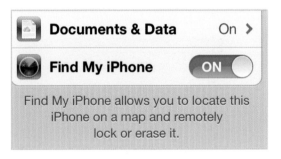

 ALERT: If a thief steals your phone and turns it off, you won't be able to find your iPhone using Find My iPhone.

1 Explore your iPhone and make calls

Introduction

Congratulations on the acquisition of your new iPhone 5! It's a wonderful phone with many unique, useful and entertaining features. It will help you stay in touch with others by phone, email, text messaging and social networks; you can tweet and remain 'linked in'; you can read Word documents and PDFs; and you can play games and relieve boredom in any number of ways. There are ways to be productive too, including incorporating calendars, managing multiple time zones, setting reminders and alarms, and reading email. And of course, there are all kinds of media to explore, from music and audiobooks; to video, movies and podcasts; to photos and slideshows; and more.

As you get to know your iPhone you'll also discover how to use Siri, your virtual assistant. You'll learn how to acquire apps and use them effectively. You'll learn how to surf the web. You'll even learn how to read books and magazines. Of course, there's no way to list everything you can do with your iPhone in a couple of paragraphs, so for now, we'll leave it at this. The obvious starting point, though, is learning the basics, including changing the wallpaper, connecting to a Wi-Fi network and using your iPhone to make calls.

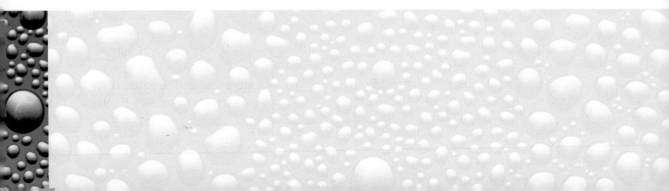

Explore the Home screen

The Home screen is the screen you see after you move the slider to unlock the iPhone. You'll see seventeen icons on the main part of the screen, and four running across the bottom in an area called the Dock. Take time to view each icon and note its name.

1 Press the Home button. This is the round, physical button located on the phone itself.

2 Move the slider from left to right to unlock the phone.

3 Note the icons on the Home screen.

? DID YOU KNOW?
A number beside an app means new information is available (an app update, an email, a missed phone call, and so on).

! ALERT: If you tap and hold any icon for two or three seconds, all of the icons will start to jiggle, ready to be edited in some way. If this happens, press the Home button.

4 Tap the phone icon and then tap the Keypad tab.

5 Press the Home button to return to the Home screen.

🔥 **HOT TIP:** When opened, some apps (such as Weather), may ask for permission to use your current location to personalise the data provided (in this case, to give you the status of your local weather). It's almost always OK to agree to this.

Explore the outside of your iPhone

The most used item on the iPhone itself is the Home button. This is the round button located at the bottom of the iPhone when it is facing you (while holding it in portrait mode). You press this to access the Lock screen (where the slider is) and to return to the Home screen when you're finished using an app. Beyond the Home button there are other items to explore.

1 The Lightning connector – Located at the bottom of the iPhone; used to charge the iPhone and physically connect it to your computer.

2 Camera lenses – Located at the top of the front and back of the iPhone; used to take pictures and video, and communicate with FaceTime.

3 Headphone jack – Located at the bottom of the iPhone; used to connect headphones and other compatible sound devices.

4 On/Off/Sleep button – Located at the top of the iPhone; used to lock the phone, turn it off and turn it on.

5 Volume buttons – Located on the left side of the iPhone; used to increase or decrease the volume, or to mute the iPhone quickly. You'll see a visual on the screen when changing the volume.

? DID YOU KNOW?

While viewing the Home screen, you can double-press the Home button to flick through available apps. From the Lock screen, you can double-press to access the Music controls.

🔥 HOT TIP: Press and hold the Home button to access Siri, your digital assistant. Press again to close the Siri dialog.

Change the wallpaper

Your iPhone comes with lots of wallpaper you can choose from, and you can use pictures you've taken or otherwise acquired on it as well. The first step in personalising your iPhone is to change the wallpaper. (This task offers a great way to explore the Settings app too.)

1 From the Home screen, tap Settings.

2 Tap Brightness & Wallpaper; and tap the two Wallpaper thumbnails in the resulting screen to access the wallpaper options.

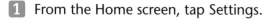

WHAT DOES THIS MEAN?
Wallpaper: the picture you see on the Lock screen and on the Home screen. You can have different wallpaper for each.

3 Tap Wallpaper again.

4 Tap any wallpaper in the list then tap Set.

5 Opt to set the wallpaper for the Lock Screen, Home Screen, or both.

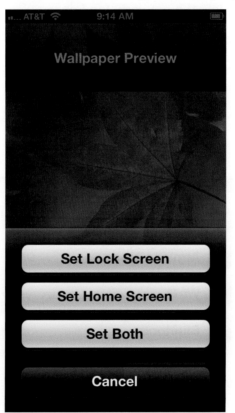

6 Repeat if desired; press the Home button when finished.

ALERT: The next time you open the Settings app, it will open to the last place you left off (perhaps the Wallpaper screen). If this happens, you'll have to tap the appropriate 'back' buttons to return to the main Settings screen.

Connect to a Wi-Fi network

When you want to connect to the Internet, your iPhone first attempts to connect through a free Wi-Fi network. If it can't find one, it will use your cellular data network. Because you have to pay for the latter, and because you likely have a limited data plan, it's in your best interest to connect to Wi-Fi networks whenever they are available.

1 Get within range of a known Wi-Fi network, such as one at your home, or at a local library, pub, cafe or hotel.

2 If you are prompted to join the network, tap Join.

3 If required to type a password, do so.

4 If you are not prompted to join a known Wi-Fi network:
   ● Tap Settings.
   ● Tap any required 'back' buttons to return to the main Settings screen.
   ● Tap Wi-Fi (it will show Not Connected).

? DID YOU KNOW?
Wi-Fi networks are almost always noticeably faster than cellular networks.

! ALERT: Wi-Fi must be enabled to connect to networks. If applicable, turn Airplane Mode off and Wi-Fi on.

- Tap the desired network to connect to.
- Type a password if applicable.

5 By default, Ask to Join Networks is turned off. Turn on if desired.

HOT TIP: When you want to download apps, movies and media, make sure you're connected to Wi-Fi; otherwise you'll use up your monthly quota data quickly.

Understand iCloud

iCloud is a place on the Internet where you can store data. Apple provides 5 GB of iCloud space for you to use, for free. When you store data in iCloud, you can access all of it from other iDevices, and some of it (Mail, Contacts, Calendars and so on) from almost any Internet-connected computer, tablet or laptop.

- iCloud has its own tab in Settings.

- iCloud offers an easy way to back up important data, such as contacts, notes, bookmarks and photos you take with the iPhone's camera.

- You can opt out of iCloud if you like, or only store specific data there.

- When you use iCloud with multiple iDevices, changes you save to iCloud can be synced to other devices easily. If you make a change to a contact on your iPhone, for instance, that change can be sent to your iPad automatically.

HOT TIP: Set up Find My iPhone as soon as possible. This is available from the iCloud options from Settings. This will help you find your phone should it go missing, provided it is turned on.

- Some data you store in iCloud can be accessed from any computer that is connected to the Internet at www.icloud.com.

Enable or disable iCloud

You must enable iCloud if you want to use it, although it may already be enabled and you simply don't know it! When you enable iCloud you can pick and choose what you want to store and back up there.

1 Tap Settings on the Home screen.

2 Tap any 'back' buttons as required to return to the main Settings screen.

3 Tap iCloud.

4 From the iCloud options, choose what to sync and what not to.

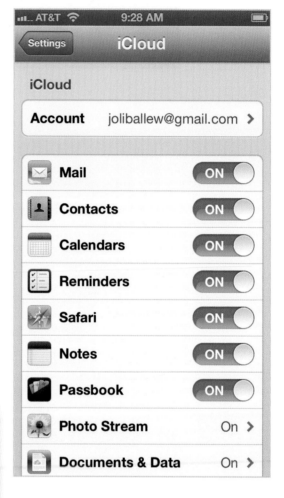

HOT TIP: When you turn on Photo Stream, you can store up to 1,000 photos in iCloud. If you go over that limit, older photos will 'roll off' to make room for newer ones. To keep all of your photos, also sync your iPhone with your computer regularly.

ALERT: If you sync your iPhone to your computer using iTunes, be careful what you also sync to iCloud, and vice versa. If you sync, say, your contacts to both, you may end up with duplicates and conflicts on your iPhone since your contact data comes from two different places.

DID YOU KNOW?
If you have multiple iDevices that are iCloud compatible, items you store in iCloud can be synced to those other devices automatically.

Install iTunes on your computer

You use iTunes on your computer to sync your iPhone with it. When you do, you create a backup as well. You can also use iTunes to copy media from your computer to your iPhone to populate it with media. You'll want to do this if you have music, movies, videos, personal photos, audiobooks and other media on your computer that you'd like also to have on your iPhone.

1 From your computer, visit www.apple.com/itunes.

2 Locate and click the download option for the latest iTunes download.

3 Follow the instructions to complete the download and installation process; this will vary depending on your web browser and operating system.

 HOT TIP: Even if you use iCloud to back up your data, you should still set up iTunes on your computer and back it up there too. Just make sure not to sync specific data to both.

4 Open iTunes after it's installed and wait for it to locate and import your media.

Perform your first sync

You may have songs on your computer you'd like to have on your iPhone, or you may have movies, audiobooks, photos or other data. To copy this type of data to your iPhone, you must sync it to your computer.

1 Connect your iPhone to your computer using the USB cable that came with it.

2 Click your iPhone on the left side of iTunes.

3 Click each tab, specifically Music and Photos, and select items you'd like to have on your iPhone.

4 Keep an eye on the bar that runs across the bottom of the iTunes interface, denoting how full your iPhone will be if you sync the selected media.

5 Once you've selected the desired media, click Sync.

ALERT: Leave enough room on your iPhone to take pictures, acquire apps, store books and obtain media.

WHAT DOES THIS MEAN?

Sync: When you sync two devices, you are making sure that the same data appears on both, as you've configured it to. If you make a change on one device later, when you sync again the change will be applied to the other.

Enable iTunes Wi-Fi sync

You can sync your iPhone with your computer automatically over Wi-Fi without physically connecting it, provided certain criteria are met. You enable this from iTunes on your computer, from the Summary tab, while your iPhone is connected.

1 In iTunes, from the Summary tab, enable Sync with this iPhone over Wi-Fi. Click Apply. (Apply won't be available if criteria can't be met by your computer or network.)

Backup

○ Back up to iCloud
○ Back up to this computer
☐ Encrypt local backup [Change Password...]
Last backed up to iCloud: Today 8:41 AM

Options

1
☑ Open iTunes when this iPhone is connected
☑ Sync with this iPhone over Wi-Fi
☐ Sync only checked songs and videos
☐ Prefer standard definition videos
☐ Convert higher bit rate songs to [128 kbps ♦] AAC
☐ Manually manage music and videos

2 Detach your iPhone from the computer.

3 Plug your iPhone into an electrical outlet.

4 Verify the computer is turned on and iTunes is running.

5 Tap Settings > General > iTunes Wi-Fi Sync, and tap Sync now.

? DID YOU KNOW?
When these criteria are met, your iPhone will sync automatically and without prompting or intervention once a day.

! ALERT: The computer and the iPhone must be connected to the same Wi-Fi network you used to configure Wi-Fi syncing.

Place and receive calls

You place calls from the Home screen. Just tap the green phone icon that sits on the Dock. There are five tabs to choose from: Favorites, Recents, Contacts, Keypad, Voicemail.

1 To place a call:
- Tap the phone icon.
- Tap the Keypad tab.
- Type the phone number.
- Tap Call.

2 To receive a call, tap Answer if the phone is active, or use the slider to answer the call if the phone is not.

3 To decline a call, tap Decline if the phone is active, or drag the phone icon on the Lock screen upward to see other options.

4 If you miss or decline a call, a number will appear on the phone icon.

 **HOT TIP:** To make the number on the phone icon disappear, tap it and then tap Recents. This icon represents the number of missed and declined calls.

? DID YOU KNOW?
The screen you see when you tap the phone icon is the last screen you accessed when you used the phone.

 **HOT TIP:** If you can't answer a call but want to acknowledge it, tap Reply with Message. You can send a text to the caller to let them know you'll call them back shortly. There are several default messages you can choose from if you don't want to type your own.

View the call log

You access your recent incoming, outgoing and missed calls from the Recents tab. From there you can return a call with a single tap, add a caller to your Contacts list, delete calls from the list and sort the list by all calls or by missed calls only.

Tap the phone icon and then Recents, then:

1 Tap All or Missed to filter calls.

2 Tap Edit and then tap the red line next to any call to delete it from the list. (Tap Done when finished.)

3 Tap the name or number of a caller to return the call.

..... AT&T 📶	10:23 AM	🔋
	All Missed	Edit
Joli Ballew (7) home	10:12 AM	❯
Joli Ballew home	10:02 AM	❯
Joli Ballew home	10:01 AM	❯
Unknown unknown	9:11 AM	❯
Jennifer and Andrew... mobile	9/19/12	❯
Mary Anne Cosmo mobile	9/19/12	❯
Voice Mail BHC mobile ↙	9/18/12	❯
Marine Guy mobile	9/18/12	❯
Karen Fagg work ↙	9/17/12	❯
Andre and Janice Vors... mobile ↙	9/17/12	❯
First Baptist Church		

⭐ Favorites   🕐④ Recents   👤 Contacts   ⠿ Keypad   ◉◉ Voicemail

Clear	All Missed	Done
⊖ **Joli Ballew** (2) home	12:20 PM	
⊖ **Dad** (4) mobile ↙	12:08 PM	

2

HOT TIP: Use the Recents list to call contacts that you communicate with often; their name will probably be in the list and you only need to tap their name to place a call.

▶ **SEE ALSO:** The section Create and edit phone contacts, later in this chapter. (You'll tap the blue arrow next to a phone number or name to get started.)

Set up voicemail

Voicemail is your iPhone's 'answering machine'. Once set up, people will be able to leave a message on it when you can't answer the phone (or when you decline a call). You set up voicemail from the Voicemail tab in the Phone app.

1 Tap the phone icon on the Home screen; tap the Voicemail tab.

2 If voicemail has not been set up, you'll be prompted on how to do this. (You'll have to create a PIN, among other things.)

3 Tap Greeting then choose from a default greeting, which will offer only your phone number, or create a custom greeting by recording your own message.

HOT TIP: Consider creating a custom greeting so that people can be sure they've reached you and not someone else.

4 Tap Play to hear your greeting. Re-record if desired.

5 Tap Save. Now you can tap the Voicemail tab to retrieve messages.

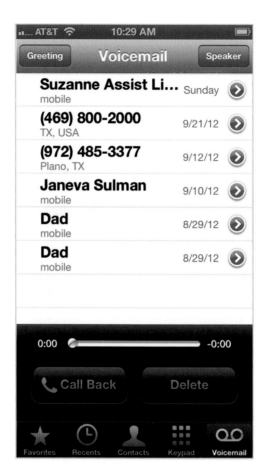

? **DID YOU KNOW?**

You can change the greeting at any time by tapping Greeting from the Voicemail tab.

Listen to your voicemail

When you miss a call and the caller leaves a message, you'll see a prompt on your iPhone the next time you press the Home button. You'll also see a number on the phone icon, and if you open the app, you'll see a number on the Voicemail tab too.

1 Tap the phone icon on the Home screen.

2 Tap the Voicemail tab.

3 Tap the entry for the voicemail you want to hear.

4 If desired, tap Speaker.

5 Listen to the message. If desired, tap Delete or Call Back. You can also listen to your message again by tapping it.

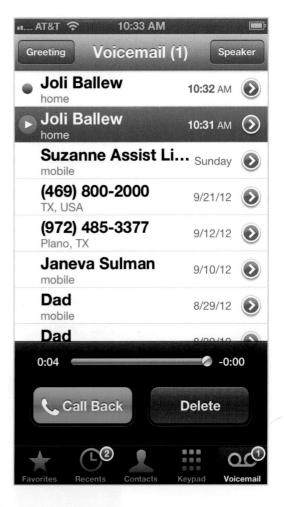

? DID YOU KNOW?
You can pause the playback of a voicemail by tapping the entry.

HOT TIP: There's no reason to delete a voicemail right away, especially if you think you'll need to listen to it again. When new messages arrive, they'll appear at the top of the list.

HOT TIP: Tap the blue arrow by any number in the Voicemail list to access options, including one to create a contact or add the number to an existing contact.

Create and edit phone contacts

You can create a contact from the Contacts tab by tapping the + sign on that screen. You can add a contact from any number from any calling list as well, by tapping the blue arrow beside the number and tapping Create New Contact. Whatever you choose, a New Contact card will open and you will populate it with data.

To create a new contact from scratch:

1 In the phone app, tap the Contacts tab.

2 If applicable, tap any 'back' buttons to access the screen that holds the + sign.

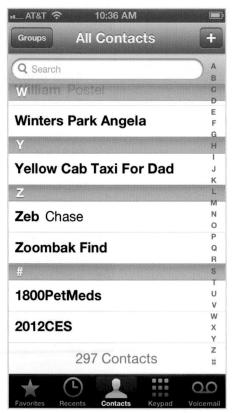

DID YOU KNOW?

You can tap an existing contact name in the Contacts list (Contacts tab), tap Edit, and re-enter or add information as warranted.

3 Tap the + sign.

4 Tap and then type the desired information.

5 Tap Done.

HOT TIP: Edit any contact and configure it as a 'favorite' and their contact information will appear on the Favorites tab.

HOT TIP: Tap Add Photo to take or select a picture for the contact.

Access and use in-call options

When you are on a call you will occasionally need to do something else at the same time. Perhaps you need to put someone on hold, 'Press 1 to continue', add someone to the call or look up contact information. You can do all of this and more. The screen that holds these options appears automatically when you remove the phone from your ear.

1 Mute – in essence, to put the call on hold by muting your outgoing speaker. When mute is enabled, you can continue to talk (perhaps to a colleague in the same room) but the person on the other end of the line can't hear what you are saying.

2 Keypad – To access the keypad in order to press a number as prompted by an operator. Tap Hide Keypad to return to the controls.

3 Speaker – To place the call on speaker, so you can free your hands for other tasks or to let others around you hear the conversation.

4 Add call – To add another caller to the conversation.

5 FaceTime – To switch to a FaceTime conversation.

6 Contacts – To access your Contacts list, perhaps to look up contact information.

SEE ALSO: For more information about FaceTime, refer to Chapter 8.

HOT TIP: If you get a lot of phone calls, consider a hands-free Bluetooth headset.

2 Learn iPhone basics

Introduction

You can use your iPhone for many things. You can take pictures and view them. You can check the weather in your area or elsewhere. You can tell Siri, your virtual assistant, to set an alarm, get directions or otherwise help you perform some of the tasks necessary to get through the day. Of course, you can personalise your iPhone in lots of ways too. You can configure the sounds it makes when notifications are available or a phone call arrives, move apps around, and create folders to hold apps that are alike.

In this chapter you'll learn about these areas of your iPhone and others, and what you learn here can be applied to other Home screens, apps you use and tasks you perform. These are your iPhone basics.

Move apps to different Home screens

If you do not like the current placement of your app icons, you can move them. You can reposition them on the same screen or you can drag them to a new Home screen.

1 Tap and hold any icon until they all start to jiggle.

2 Drag the icon to a new area of the same screen or off the screen to another one.

3 Let go of the icon to drop it there. (Don't drop it on top of another icon!)

4 Repeat as desired.

5 Press the Home button to apply changes.

ALERT: If you drop one icon on top of another, a folder will be created that holds both. Drag the icon out of the folder to undo this change. Make sure not to drag the icon on top of another when letting it go next time.

SEE ALSO: The section Create folders for apps, towards the end of this chapter.

Take a photo

The camera icon is positioned on the main Home screen of your iPhone. You tap it to open the camera and take pictures. The Camera screen has several features; to take a basic photo you simply select the front- or rear-facing still camera and tap the shutter icon.

1. Auto – Tap to turn on or off the flash. Leave this to its Auto setting to let your iPhone decide what is best for each shot.

2. Options – To turn on the grid for framing the shot, High Dynamic Range for higher quality pictures, and Panorama, for taking a panoramic picture.

3. Switch lenses – To switch from the front- to rear-facing lenses and back again.

4. Thumbnail – To see the last picture taken (and to open the Photos app).

5. Shutter – To take a picture.

6. Camera mode – To switch from the still camera to the video camera.

HOT TIP: To take a video instead of a still picture, move the slider on the bottom right to the video camera, and use the shutter button to start and then stop recording.

DID YOU KNOW?
You can tap the screen once to denote what you'd like the camera to focus on while capturing the shot.

View your photos

The Photos app offers access to your photos. Once in the app, you can select a photo category and then flick left and right to move among the photos there.

1 From the Home screen, tap Photos.

2 If you do not see something similar to what is shown here, tap the 'back' button until you do. (There is no 'back' button available here.)

	AT&T 📶	7:10 AM	🔋
+		**Albums**	Edit

Camera Roll (330) >

Photo Library (860) >

Allison Favorites (22) >

Friends (31) >

Houses (298) >

Me, Jennifer, Mom,... (190) >

My Favorites (60) >

Pets (144) >

Albums | Photo Stream | Places

? DID YOU KNOW?

The Photo Stream tab at the bottom only offers photos taken from the iDevices you use and have configured to save to Photo Stream.

3 Make sure Albums is selected at the bottom, then tap Camera Roll; tap the photo to view.

Note the controls available (tap the screen if the controls go missing):

4 The 'back' button, to return to the previous screen.

5 The Edit button to fix the photo.

6 The Share icon to access sharing options.

7 The option to play a slideshow.

8 The Trash icon to delete the picture.

? **DID YOU KNOW?**

While in the Camera app you can tap the thumbnail to see the most recently taken snapshot.

Use the Weather app

One of the apps on the Home screen is Weather. Tap it, and if the app asks for permission to use your current location, allow it. Once the app has opened, you can view your local weather and configure additional locations for weather information.

1 Tap the Weather app to open it. Your local weather should appear.

2 Flick from right to left on the screen to access the forecast for other cities (Cupertino is shown here).

HOT TIP: If you opted not to let the Weather app learn your location and now you want it to, from the Home screen, tap Settings, Privacy, then tap Location Services. You can now specify which apps can access your current location and which can't.

3 Tap the small *i* in the bottom right corner; the page will 'flip' to the other side.

4 Tap the + sign on the next screen. (You can tap the red dashes and delete what's there if you like.)

5 Type the name of a city, tap Search, and tap the desired result in the list that appears.

6 Tap Done.

Set an alarm

You can set an alarm manually, although you can ask Siri to do it for you if you'd rather. (You'll learn about Siri in Chapter 3.) Here you'll learn how to set an alarm manually, which is a good way to get to know the Clock app.

1 From the Home screen, tap Clock.

2 Note the tabs; tap Alarm.

3 Tap the + sign.

ALERT: You can only set an alarm for a time that is less than 24 hours from the current time. If you want to set an alarm for say, sometime next week, you'll have to create a reminder instead.

4 Tap, flick, click or swipe to set the time for the alarm.

5 Tap Save.

Get directions to a location

You use the Maps app to locate places on a map and get directions. If you want directions from your current location, simply type where you'd like to go in the Search or Address window and tap Search on the keyboard. If you want to name your starting point or if the directions you receive don't start at your current location, you'll have to follow the steps here.

1 Tap Maps, and tap the right-facing arrow at the top of the screen.

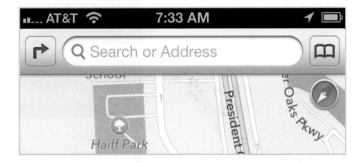

2 Type your Start and End points. You may be able to type business names, landmarks, and so on.

3 Tap any result or tap Route.

4 If necessary, pinch outward to view the results.

5 Tap the red pin that denotes the location you're looking for.

6 If desired, tap the blue arrow for even more information. For turn-by-turn directions, tap Start.

HOT TIP: If prompted to let Maps use your current location, tap OK.

? DID YOU KNOW?
You can type an address or the name of a business in the Search window.

Set a reminder with Siri

A reminder is an element of a to-do list. Once reminders are set they are available from the Reminders app and the Notification pull-down list (detailed later). The easiest way to set a reminder is to ask Siri to do it.

1 Tap and hold the Home button.

2 When the microphone icon turns purple say, 'Remind me'. If it is not purple, tap it.

3 Answer Siri's questions. You can say something like, 'I have a meeting tomorrow'.

4 Continue to answer Siri's questions, and when prompted, say 'Yes' to confirm.

5 Note the reminder (do not check it off here). Tap the Home screen to close Siri.

! ALERT: You must be able to access the Internet to use Siri. You must also have enabled Siri in Settings > General > Siri.

? DID YOU KNOW?
You can put your entire request into a single sentence, like 'Remind me to pick up the dry cleaning tomorrow at 2 p.m.'

HOT TIP: To view today's reminders, pull downwards from the top of the screen. You'll see your reminder there.

Learn how to dictate text

You already know how to talk to Siri. You can also use your voice to dictate text instead of typing it. Whenever a keyboard is available, a microphone appears on it. Tap the microphone to dictate. An easy way to learn how to dictate is to practise with the Notes app.

 Tap the Notes app on the Home screen.

2 Tap the + sign to start a new note.

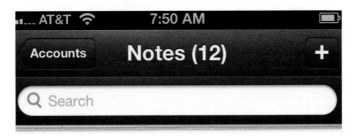

3 Tap the microphone on the screen and start talking. Add punctuation as needed.

4 Tap Done to stop dictating and add the text.

5 Use the keyboard to fix any problems. You can use the Back key, or you can tap, hold and drag to place the cursor anywhere.

HOT TIP: You'll have to state the punctuation you want inserted, otherwise what is dictated will appear as a single, long text entry.

6 Continue dictating as desired, until you are comfortable with the process.

7 Tap Done, then tap Notes to return to the Notes list.

Personalise sounds

When a phone call arrives, a certain ringtone is played. Likewise, a specific tone plays when you receive a new email or text, receive a voicemail, send a tweet, and more. You can change all of these sounds and others from the Settings app. You can even personalise the vibrations the phone makes when a phone call comes in.

1 On the Home screen, tap Settings.

2 Tap any 'back' buttons as required to access the main Settings screen. Tap Sounds.

.ıl... AT&T 📶	7:54 AM	🔋
	Settings	
🔘 **General**		>
🔊 **Sounds**		>
🌸 **Brightness & Wallpaper**		>
✋ **Privacy**		>
☁️ **iCloud**		>
✉️ **Mail, Contacts, Calendars**		>
📓 **Notes**		>
📋 **Reminders**		>

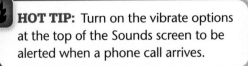

HOT TIP: Turn on the vibrate options at the top of the Sounds screen to be alerted when a phone call arrives.

3 Scroll down to the notification types. You can see Ringtone and Text Tone here, but there are more.

	7:54 AM	
..... AT&T 📶		🔋

‹ Settings   Sounds

Vibrate

Vibrate on Ring	ON ⬤

Vibrate on Silent	ON ⬤

Ringer and Alerts

🔈 ━━━━━⬤━━━━━ 🔊

Change with Buttons	ON ⬤

The volume of the ringer and alerts can be adjusted using the volume buttons.

Sounds and Vibration Patterns

Ringtone	Marimba ›
Text Tone	Tri-tone ›
New Voicemail	Tri-tone ›

4 To change the vibration pattern or create your own, tap the entry next to Vibration and make the appropriate choices. Tap the Sounds back button. To change a tone, tap it and select a different tone.

5 Tap Sounds to return to the Sounds screen (and Settings to return to the Settings screen).

? DID YOU KNOW?
You can change the default sounds for many features including new voicemail, email, sent mail, tweets, alerts, and more.

View notifications

Notifications such as today's reminders, Calendar app alerts, Messenger texts, and information provided by apps (it's your turn in a multiplayer game perhaps), can be viewed from the Notifications pull-down screen. You can also configure additional information to appear, such as your local weather (from Settings > Notifications).

1 From any screen, tap and hold the top bar of the screen (where the time appears is a good place to do this).

2 Drag this toolbar downwards.

3 Note the notifications.

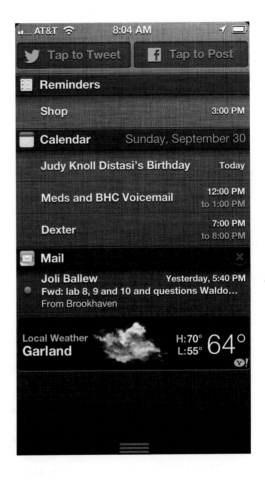

 HOT TIP: Change which notifications appear in the Notifications area from Settings > Notifications. Learn how in the next section.

Personalise notifications

You may see notifications in the Notifications pull-down list that you don't need to see. You may need to add items as well. You can personalise what shows there in the Settings app.

1 From the Home screen, tap Settings.

2 Tap Notifications.

3 To view the notifications listed in the order they arrived, tap By Time.

? DID YOU KNOW?

You can scroll down to the bottom of the Notifications screen to view apps that do not offer information in the Notifications area. You can set them to do so, if desired.

HOT TIP: Configure Do Not Disturb settings so that when you enable the feature it will work the way you want it to. Do Not Disturb lets you block incoming calls except from the people in your Favorites list, among other things.

4 To remove a particular type of notification, click it in the In Notification Center section.

5 Select to show the item in the Notifications area or not, and what type of alert to associate with it.

6 Tap Notifications to return to the previous screen.

Connect a Bluetooth device

A Bluetooth device is one that you can connect to your iPhone and that can communicate with it wirelessly. You may have a hands-free headset that fits this category. These headsets (or earpieces) enable you to answer phone calls without touching your iPhone or even looking at it.

1 Turn on the Bluetooth device you want to connect.

2 On your iPhone, tap Settings and then Bluetooth.

3 Move the slider from off to on.

4 When the iPhone finds the device, tap it.

5 Follow the rest of the instructions to pair the device. Here, a keyboard is paired.

ALERT: Turn off Bluetooth when you don't need it. Bluetooth can drain your battery.

? DID YOU KNOW?
There are lots of kinds of Bluetooth devices, including keyboards. If you are in the market for one, make sure it's iPhone 5 compatible before you buy it.

HOT TIP: When you finish configuring settings in the Settings app, tap the 'back' button the necessary number of times to return to the main Settings screen. This will make the settings quickly available next time you need them.

Learn more touch techniques

You know quite a few touch techniques already, and you'll learn more as you work through this text. To whet your appetite, here are a few to experiment with now.

1 From any home screen, flick from left to right until you can't flick any more. This is the Search screen.

2 Flick from right to left to see additional Home screens.

3 Tap Phone, tap Contacts, and flick up and down to move through your contacts quickly.

HOT TIP: Apply these techniques to other apps you use. Many let you pinch and scroll to navigate data.

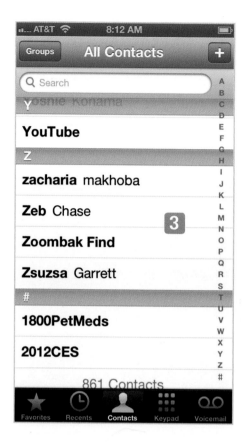

4 From the Home screen, tap Maps then flick up and down, and pinch out and in.

5 From the Home screen, tap Stocks, and flick left and right at the bottom of the screen to view information.

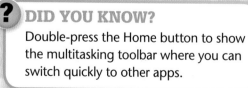

? DID YOU KNOW?

Double-press the Home button to show the multitasking toolbar where you can switch quickly to other apps.

Type with the keyboard

You can tap keys on the keyboard to type; that's easy. You probably know that the up arrow is the Shift key. But you should also know how to enable Caps Lock and perform various keyboard shortcuts.

1. Double-tap the Space key to add a full stop and end a sentence while typing.

2. To add a comma, tap and hold the 123 key and slide your finger to the comma.

3. Tap the up arrow twice to enable Caps Lock. Tap once to disable.

4. Touch and hold the compatible keys to access other entries.

5. Tap and hold the letter O (among others) to access additional characters.

! ALERT: Keyboard features should be enabled by default in Settings > General > Keyboard, but it doesn't hurt to check, just to be sure.

? DID YOU KNOW? You can enable an international keyboard in the Settings app.

Create folders for apps

You can tap, hold and then drag apps to a new position on the screen or to another Home screen. If you want to group two or more apps together, because they are alike or because you don't use them, you can use a similar technique to place them together. This isn't for the faint of heart!

1 Tap and hold the Reminders app until all of the apps start to jiggle.

2 Drop the Reminders app onto the Notes app and note the new folder.

3 Press the Home button twice to apply the change.

! ALERT: Moving and grouping apps is a little tricky and takes some practice. If you don't want to do this right now, you can always come back to it later.

? DID YOU KNOW?
You can rename a folder by tapping the X there and typing a new name.

4 To undo this:

- Tap the folder to open it. Tap and hold the Reminders app until all the apps start to jiggle.

- Drag the Reminders app out of the folder and back to its original position.
- Tap the Home button to apply the change. Repeat to remove the Notes app and get rid of the new folder.
- Tap the Home button to apply the changes.

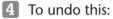

Set a passcode lock

You should create and apply a passcode lock to protect your iPhone. A passcode lock is a four-digit number you must input after moving the slider on the Lock screen. You won't be able to access the Home screen (and thus your iPhone data) until you input this number.

1 Tap Settings and then tap General.

2 Tap Passcode Lock.

.ıl... AT&T 🛜	8:22 AM	🔋
‹ Settings	**General**	

Spotlight Search	›

Auto-Lock	3 Minutes ›
Passcode Lock	Off ›
Restrictions	Off ›

Date & Time	›
Keyboard	›
International	›
Accessibility	›

Reset	›

 HOT TIP: If you decide later to set 'restrictions' so your children can't use certain programs when they have your iPhone, make sure you configure a different passcode from the one you configure here.

3 Tap Turn Passcode On and enter a four-digit passcode you can remember. Input it again when prompted.

4 Change Require Passcode to Immediately.

5 Tap the Home button.

```
.ıl... AT&T 🔊          8:23 AM          ▭

⟨ General   Passcode Lock


      Turn Passcode Off

      Change Passcode

                                    4
Require Passcode    Immediately  ❯

Simple Passcode          ON ◯

   A simple passcode is a 4 digit number.

Allow Access When Locked:

Siri                     ON ◯

Passbook                 ON ◯

Reply with Message       ON ◯


Erase Data               ◯ OFF

      Erase all data on this iPhone
```

? **DID YOU KNOW?**

Auto-Lock is another option from Settings > General. Use this to configure how long your iPhone should remain idle before it locks itself automatically.

3 Meet Siri

Introduction

Siri is your digital assistant. You can ask Siri to tell you the current time, your present location and the current weather conditions, and more. You have already learned how to ask Siri to set a reminder for you (see Chapter 2), but there's so much more you can do.

As an example, you can tell Siri to play a song, place a call, cancel a meeting, set an alarm, get directions, and so on. You can have Siri surf the Internet when he doesn't know the answer offhand. And you can even have a bit of fun with Siri. Want to try it out? Ask Siri to tell you a joke!

You must be connected to the Internet to use Siri.

Enable Siri and choose a language

You must enable Siri in order to use the feature. When you do, you can then choose a language and configure other options.

 From the Home screen, tap Settings.

 Tap General, and then tap Siri.

 Turn Siri on.

 If desired:

- Choose a different language from the one that is configured.
- Choose when Siri should offer voice feedback (always, or only when you're 'hands free').
- Tell Siri which contact card is yours.
- Configure Siri to work when you tap and hold the Home button *and* when you hold the phone to your ear (when not in a call), if desired.

ALERT: You must be connected to the Internet to use Siri.

? DID YOU KNOW?
There are two ways to wake Siri if you turn on Raise to Speak. You can tap and hold the Home button or you can raise the phone to your ear when it's unlocked.

Tell Siri your name

Siri may already know your name, but you should tell him anyway (yes, we'll personify Siri in this text) just to make sure he knows exactly who you are. You may want Siri to call you something else instead. You can have Siri call you anything you like!

1 Tap and hold the Home button until the microphone icon appears.

2 Say, 'Siri, call me <and state what you'd like to be called here>'. You might say, 'Siri, call me The Big Kahuna'.

3 If Siri responds correctly, say 'OK' or tap Yes.

4 If Siri does not respond correctly, click or say 'Cancel'.

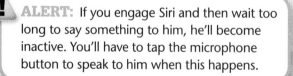

ALERT: If you engage Siri and then wait too long to say something to him, he'll become inactive. You'll have to tap the microphone button to speak to him when this happens.

ALERT: Be careful when you speak to Siri and start a sentence with 'call me'. For instance, if you say to Siri, *'Call me an ambulance'*, he will probably respond with 'OK, from now on I'll call you An Ambulance'. That's probably not what you want.

? DID YOU KNOW?
If you say to Siri, 'Siri, call Bob', Siri will look for Bob in your contacts and ring him. If you say to Siri, 'Siri, call *me* Bob', Siri will say something like, 'OK, from now on I'll call you Bob'.

Have Siri place a call

It generally takes two hands to place a phone call. You need one to hold the phone and the other to punch in the numbers (unless you are dexterous enough to dial with your thumb while you hold the phone with your other fingers). You can place a call with one hand if Siri is enabled and if the person you want to call is in your Contacts list.

1 Tap and hold the Home button until the microphone icon appears.

2 Say, 'Siri, call <and state the name of the contact to call>'.

3 If Siri can't find the contact, you'll see a message something like the one shown here.

> I don't see 'Steffano' in your address book. Should I look for businesses by that name?
>
> Find businesses named 'Steffano'

4 If Siri finds the contact, he'll inform you he's placing the call.

> Calling FedEx's mobile phone:
> 1 (800) 463-3339...

HOT TIP: If more than one phone number exists for a contact, Siri will ask you which number to ring.

? DID YOU KNOW?
Siri prefers that you speak slowly and carefully.

Let Siri play a song or album

If you have music on your iPhone, Siri can play it for you. You'll need to say the name of the song or album for Siri to find it. To see what songs and albums are available, tap the Music app and tap Songs or tap Albums.

1 Tap and hold the Home button.

2 Say, 'Siri, play <and say the name of the song or album>'.

3 If the command is successful, the song or album will play.

Playing 'We Are the World'...

4 Tap Music on the Home screen to stop or pause playback.

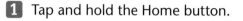

! ALERT: For Siri to play music, music tracks must be available from your iPhone.

? DID YOU KNOW?
You can also tell Siri, 'Play some country music' or 'Play some rock music'. Siri will play music in that genre.

Set up or cancel a meeting

Siri can act as your personal secretary and set up meetings for you. Just tell Siri you'd like to set up a meeting and with whom, and on what day and at which time. If you don't get all of that out in one sentence, Siri will ask you for any information you left out. Once you've scheduled the meeting, an invitation will be automatically sent to the meeting attendee(s).

1 Press and hold the Home button, and when the microphone appears, say, 'I need to schedule a meeting'.

2 Answer the questions as Siri asks you.

3 Once you've answered all of the questions, Siri will create an event.

4 Confirm the meeting when prompted.

HOT TIP: To view and edit a meeting, open the Calendar app, tap the meeting, and tap Edit. You may want to add something, such as a meeting place, phone number or room number.

? DID YOU KNOW?
You can view and edit your meeting from the Calendar app.

HOT TIP: To cancel a meeting, tell Siri, 'Cancel my meeting with <name> on <day or date>'.

? DID YOU KNOW?
When you create a meeting with a person in your Contacts list, a meeting invitation will be sent to them via email. When they reply, the meeting will be updated in the Calendar app to show their response.

Set or cancel an alarm

You have already learned how to set an alarm manually using the Clock app (see Chapter 2). It's much easier to tell Siri when you'd like to be awakened and let him set the alarm for you.

1 Press and hold the Home button. When the microphone icon appears, tell Siri, 'Set an alarm'.

2 When Siri answers, tell him what time to set the alarm for.

3 The alarm will be set.

Let Siri find an answer on the web

Siri can't answer all of your questions all of the time. In fact, Siri can provide information only if the answer is stored on your phone or can be gleaned using it. Sometimes Siri must search the Internet to offer information regarding the answers you seek. Ask Siri the following questions to get an idea of how this works and of when Siri needs to look to the Internet for answers.

1 'What time is it?' – Siri can get this information from your phone.

2 'Where am I?' – Siri can get this information from GPS and Maps.

3 'How many metres are in a mile?' – Siri can find this information from his 'sources' on the Internet, but does not have to make you browse search results.

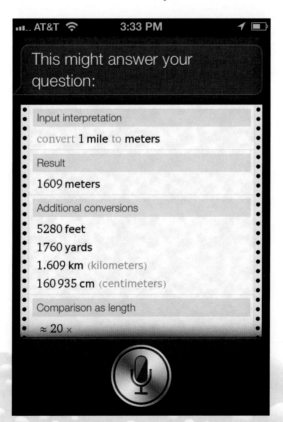

4 'What is my ideal weight?' – Siri has no way of knowing the answer and thus refers you to the web.

I can't answer that. But I could search the web for it, if you like.

Search the web

5 'Who won the <...> game last week?'

6 'Tweet something' or 'Update my Facebook status'.

? DID YOU KNOW?
Siri can answer some fairly complex questions, like 'Where is the nearest Thai restaurant that has good ratings?', by incorporating your current location, Google Maps and information on nearby eateries.

HOT TIP: Try asking Siri something silly, like 'Do you like me?'

Ask for directions, distance or your current location

Siri knows where you are (well, technically, where your phone is) and can thus calculate how far specific places are from you, including nearby cities and towns. If you ask Siri for directions to a specific place such as a hairdresser or restaurant, he'll assume (and rightly so) that you want to locate one that's nearby. He'll offer the information in Maps.

Ask Siri these questions:

1 'How far is <name the closest city> from here?'

2 'How far is <name any country> from here?'

3 'Where can I get a haircut?'

4 'Is there a Thai restaurant nearby?'

5 'Where is the nearest subway station?'

> **! ALERT:** Remember, if you engage Siri and then wait too long to say something to him, he'll become inactive. You'll have to tap the microphone button to speak to him when this happens.

> **🔥 HOT TIP:** Siri may not be able to find everything you ask for. For instance, if there are no subway stations nearby, Siri won't be able to point you to any.

> **! ALERT:** Siri may not be able to give you information about other countries!

..... AT&T 🛜   9:16 AM

I found six Thai restaurants... three of them are fairly close to you: **4**

THAI CORNER
THAI .... $$$$
5129 N GARLAND AVE .... 1.3 MI
★★★☆☆ 20 REVIEWS

THAI JASMINE
SUSHI BARS, THAI .... $$$$
5129 N GARLAND AVE .... 1.3 MI
★★★☆☆ 13 REVIEWS

SBT LAO/THAI FOOD TO GO
THAI .... $$$$
2020 W BUCKINGHAM RD .... 2.3 MI
★★★★☆ 2 REVIEWS

TOM YUM THAI
THAI .... $$$$
3313 BELT LINE RD .... 3.0 MI
★★★★☆ 36 REVIEWS

I couldn't find any subway stations. **5**

Ask for a stock price, the weather, contact information or the latest news

Continue to experiment with Siri by asking him various questions that can be answered using the apps on your iPhone. Here are a few to try.

1 'What is Apple's current stock price?'

HOT TIP: Scroll through the results offered after asking, 'What kinds of questions can I ask you, Siri', to view all of Siri's responses.

HOT TIP: If Siri doesn't seem to understand what you're asking, speak more slowly and clearly.

2 'Is it going to rain today?'

3 'What's the latest news?'

4 'What is <say a contact's name> home address?'

5 'What kinds of questions can I ask you, Siri?'

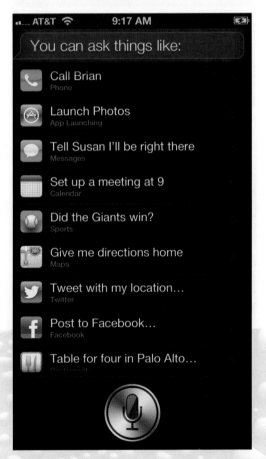

Make a note

You experimented with the Notes app when you learned how to use the keyboard (see Chapter 2). You can tell Siri to make a note too, so that you don't have to type it.

1 Say to Siri, 'Take a note'.

OK, I can take that note for you... just tell me what you want it to say.

2 Tell Siri what you'd like the note to say. Siri will write the note.

Noted:

I have some great ideas for the name of the new company

3 To see the note later, open the Notes app.

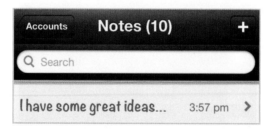

Accounts   **Notes (10)**   +

Q Search

I have some great ideas...   3:57 pm   >

🔥 **HOT TIP:** Voice Memos is an app that comes with your iPhone. You can use it to record 'voice notes'.

❓ **DID YOU KNOW?**
You can enable iCloud for Notes and have access to the notes you create on your iPhone from other iDevices you own.

Search the web for something specific

You may know by now that Siri can't answer every question you ask. You do know that Siri can't tell you what your ideal weight is! When you already know that Siri doesn't know the answer to the question you seek, you can tell Siri to go straight to the Internet for answers.

1 Tell Siri, 'Search the web'.

2 Tell Siri what you'd like to search for. I'll ask, 'How do I tie a sailor's knot?'

3 Review the results in Safari.

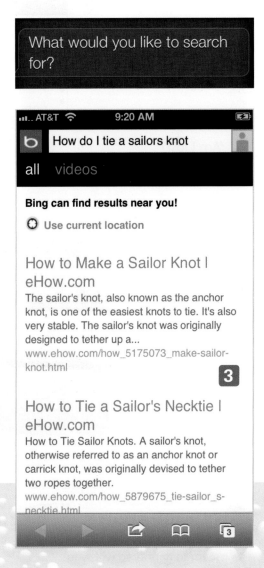

? DID YOU KNOW?
If you see the Play icon on a video clip in Safari, the video will play on your iPhone.

🔥 HOT TIP: Many pages on the web are optimised for smaller screens. If you tap a link on a web page and it's too small to read, click the Back button and try another link.

Have fun with Siri

This chapter wouldn't be complete without some 'fun with Siri'. Here are a few things to ask Siri, just for the heck of it.

1 'What is 25 × 12?'

2 'Am I lost?'

3 'Tell me a joke.'

4 'Tell me another joke.'

> Two iPhones walk into a bar... I forget the rest.

5 'Will you marry me, Siri?'

> Let's just be friends, OK?

? DID YOU KNOW?
After a round of teasing, Siri will seem to get bored with you.

🔥 HOT TIP: There are many more things you can ask Siri that weren't covered in this chapter, so experiment! For example, you can ask Siri, 'Do I have any new email?' and 'Do I have any meetings?'

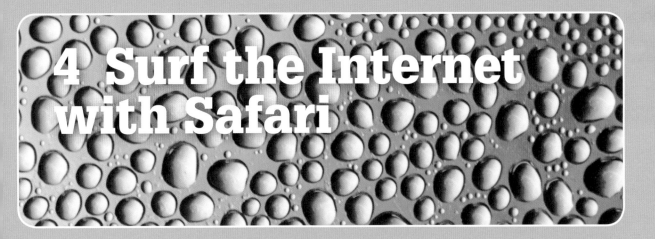

4 Surf the Internet with Safari

Introduction

Safari is the iPhone's web browser. It's on the Home screen on the Dock, and you use it to surf the Internet. Safari has much more to offer though. You can save bookmarks so you can revisit your favourite websites quickly, and you can save articles you want to read later to Safari's Reading List. You can use Safari to upload photos to websites and access the tabs saved in iCloud from all of your iDevices. You can also share what you find on the Internet in various ways or surf anonymously; it's your call.

Visit a website by typing its name

The first thing you want to do with Safari is to visit your favourite website. You can do this in quite a few ways, including clicking a link in an email or tweet. One common way is to use the keyboard to type the website's name. To get started, tap the Safari icon.

1 If this is the first time you've used Safari, you'll see a blank screen. Tap once in the *Go to this address* window.

2 If this is not the first time you've used Safari, and you see a website already:

- Tap the icon in the bottom right corner that looks like two overlapping squares.

- Tap New Page in the resulting options (not shown here).

- Tap once in the *Go to this address* window.

? **DID YOU KNOW?**

A website's name is often referred to as its address or URL (uniform resource locator).

3 Type the web address. Try Apple.com. (You don't have to type the http://www. part of the address.)

4 Tap Go.

Understand the Safari interface

You learned in the previous section that you can type a web address in the window at the top of the page, the *Go to this address* window (or just the Address window). However, there are other parts of the Safari interface to explore.

1 Search window – Tap to search for something on the web. Type keywords and then tap Go.

2 Back and Forward buttons – These become available after you've tapped links to go to new web pages and returned to previous ones.

3 Share icon – Tap to access sharing options, including, but not limited to, adding a bookmark and emailing a link to the page to someone.

4 Bookmarks icon – Tap to access your bookmarks, your Reading List, History and more, and to edit these entries.

5 New Page icon – Tap to open a new, blank page in Safari. You can also flick left and right to access other open web pages.

? DID YOU KNOW?
When you tap inside the Search window, you'll have access to your most recent searches. You can tap one to see the search results again if desired.

HOT TIP: If you can't see what's on the page because the type is too small, use a pinching motion with your thumb and forefinger to pinch outwards, and then use a single finger to scroll through information on the page.

! ALERT: Sometimes the bar that runs across the top of the Safari interface that contains the Address and Search windows disappears. This happens when you scroll down a page. Tap the very top of the Safari interface to make the bar appear again (and to return to the top of the web page quickly).

Dictate what you'd like to search for

If you only have one hand free and you need to find something on the web quickly, you can ask Siri to look it up for you. You have already learned how to ask Siri questions (see Chapter 3), and here we'll have Siri perform an internet search using a specific keyword: iPhone.

1 Press and hold the Home button.

2 When you see *What can I help you with?*, say, 'Siri, look on the Internet for iPhone'. The microphone must be purple for Siri to hear you.

3 Note the results. If desired, tap any result in the list to go to the web page.

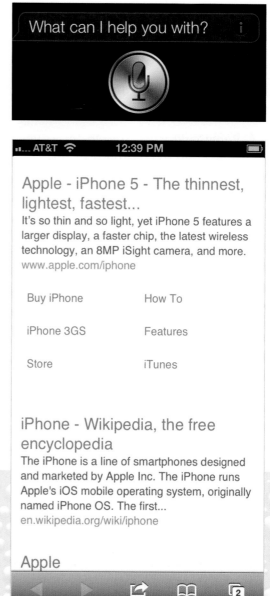

HOT TIP: If you aren't comfortable talking to Siri, do your best to overcome it. When you do things without typing, you do them faster and save wear and tear on your hands, fingers and wrists.

HOT TIP: If what you say and what Siri searches and provides results for differ, tap and hold the mouse to correct the text, or just ask Siri again.

Work with multiple open web pages

You can have multiple web pages open at one time while using Safari, but they all appear in different windows. You'll know you have multiple pages open when you see a number on the New Page icon at the bottom of the screen. When multiple web pages are open you can switch among them.

1 First, open at least one new web page:
  - Tap the New Page icon.
  - Tap New Page.
  - Navigate to any web page.

2 To switch from one open page to another:
  - Tap the New Page icon; it should have a number on it.
  - Use your finger to scroll left or right to locate the page you'd like to view.
  - Tap the page (or tap Done) to open that page.

HOT TIP: You can close any open web page by tapping the red X while in this mode.

? DID YOU KNOW?
When a web page is inactive (but still open and available), it is not being updated and it is not using your iPhone's resources. It's okay to leave multiple pages open without worry.

Create and use a bookmark

A bookmark in Safari is a shortcut to a website you visit often. You create bookmarks so that you can more easily visit your favourite websites at a later date. Once you've created a bookmark, it's easy to use it; you simply tap it in the Bookmarks list.

1 To create a bookmark:

- Navigate to a page to bookmark.
- Tap the Share icon.
- Tap Bookmark.

- If desired, rename the bookmark and tap Done or Save.

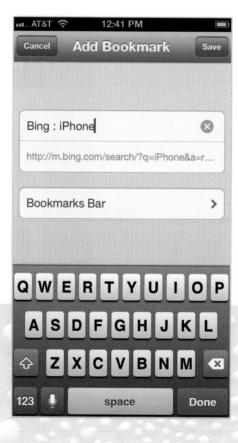

2 To access the bookmark:

- Tap the Bookmarks icon.
- Tap the desired bookmark from the list. You may have to scroll to find it.

Bookmarks	Done
📖 **Joli Amazon**	
📖 **CNN.com - Breaking Ne...**	
📖 **Sauder Cherry TV Stand...**	
📖 **Apple**	
📖 **Yahoo!**	
📖 **Google**	
📖 **Bing**	

HOT TIP: You can turn your iPhone 90 degrees left or right to view a web page in landscape mode.

? DID YOU KNOW?

You can tap Bookmarks or Bookmarks Bar (just above the keyboard) in the Add Bookmark page to select a different place to save the bookmark. You might want to choose a folder you've created. Keep reading to learn more.

Edit your Bookmarks list

When you tap the Bookmarks icon you have access to all of the bookmarks you've created. You also have access to an Edit button. When you tap Edit, you have several editing options.

1 Tap the red circle and then tap Delete to remove a bookmark. (You can also tap a folder you've created to rename it or edit it.)

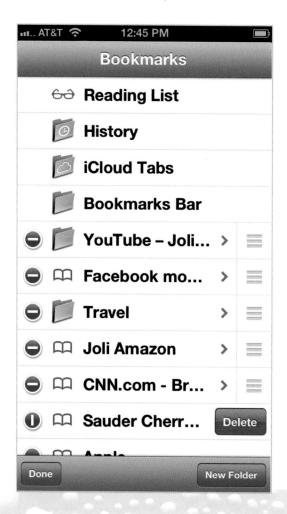

2️⃣ Tap New Folder to create a folder you can name, and then you can save new bookmarks to the folder.

3️⃣ Drag from the three horizontal lines on a bookmark to reposition it in the list.

4️⃣ Tap done to apply your changes.

HOT TIP: Before you acquire too many bookmarks, create folders. Then, when you create a new bookmark you'll already have some organisation in place, and you can save bookmarks appropriately.

ALERT: You can rename folders you've created from the appropriate Edit option; you can't rename History, iCloud Tabs, or Bookmarks Bar, though.

Add an article to the Reading List

Sometimes you'll run across an article that you don't have time to read now but would like to read later. In these cases, you save the article to the Reading List.

1 Navigate to any website. Try Wikipedia.com. (The fact that Reader appears in the Address window has nothing to do with the Reading List. See the What does this mean? box below for clarification.)

2 Locate an article you'd like to read.

3 Tap the Share button and tap Add to Reading List.

HOT TIP: You don't always have to click the New Page icon and tap New Page to navigate away from the current page to another you want to view. You can tap inside the Address window, tap the X that appears, and type the web address from there.

WHAT DOES THIS MEAN?

Reader: If you see Reader in the Address window, it means that you can view the article without ads or clutter. When you do, you can change the font size, email or print the article to a compatible printer, and more. Tap Reader to try it.

Read and share an article in the Reading List

Once you've saved items to the Reading List, you can read them when you have the time. You do not have to be connected to the Internet to access articles you've saved in the Reading List.

1 Tap the Bookmarks icon.

2 Tap Reading List.

3 Tap the article to read. (Alternatively, you can tap Done.)

Bookmarks	Done
🕶 **Reading List** 2	>
🕐 **History**	>
📁 **Bookmarks Bar**	>

.ıl. AT&T 🔋 12:53 PM 🔋

◄ Bookmarks **Reading List** Done

All | Unread

iPhone - Wikipedia, the free encyclopedia
en.m.wikipedia.org
iPhone This article is about the line of smartphones by Apple. For other uses, see iPhone (disambigua…

! ALERT: If the screen ever looks unfamiliar or you aren't sure where in the app you are, tap the 'back' button.

🔥 HOT TIP: To remove an article from the Reading List, swipe it from left to right in the list. Delete will become available, just as it does in the Mail app.

🔥 HOT TIP: When you open the Reading List, note there are two tabs, All and Unread.

Add a link for a web page to the Home screen

If you visit a website regularly, you can add an icon for it on one of your Home screens. Once it's on a Home screen, you can tap the icon to go directly to the site; you don't have to tap Safari first. As you might guess, you must first navigate to the website you'd like to add.

1 Locate the website in Safari. You might navigate to maps.google.com.

2 Tap the Share icon and tap Add to Home Screen.

© 2012 Google

3 Shorten the name of the website, if necessary, so that it's only a few letters. (This makes it easier to read on the Home screen.)

4 Tap Add.

5 Note the new icon on the Home screen.

© 2012 Google

HOT TIP: Consider creating half a dozen links to your favourite websites, and put them in a folder or on a Home screen of their own.

ALERT: If the name of the web page you've saved is too long and you'd like to shorten it, the easiest way is to delete the icon and recreate it in Safari.

Tweet or email web page information

If you find something on the Internet you want to share, tap the Share button. You'll see several choices. Two of these are Tweet and Mail Link to this Page. You can also send information in a message, share it with Facebook, and more, depending on how you've set up your iPhone.

1 Twitter – To send a link to the current web page to Twitter, to be sent out through your Twitter account. If you don't have an account or have not yet logged in with it, you'll be prompted. Then you can type your message and click Send.

2 Mail – To send a link to the current web page in an email. You have to have previously set up Mail for this to work.

.ıl.. AT&T ⏦   12:58 PM   ◢ ▭

| Cancel | **Google Maps** | Send |

To: ⊕

Cc/Bcc, From: joliballew@gmail.com

Subject: Google Maps

http://maps.google.com/#bmb=1

Sent from my iPhone

Q W E R T Y U I O P

A S D F G H J K L

⇧ Z X C V B N M ⌫

123 🎤   space   @ . return

▶ **SEE ALSO:** Chapter 5, Communicate with Mail.

🔥 **HOT TIP:** From the Share options, try Facebook, Print, and Copy, as applicable.

Explore touch techniques

You can use the same touch techniques you have already learned to move around in Safari.

1 Tap – To open a link to go to another web page; to control video; to open Share and Bookmarks options; to use the Back and Forward buttons; and so on.

2 Tap the top of Safari – To go to the top of the page quickly and to show the Address window.

3 Pinch – When applicable, to zoom in or out of a web page.

4 Double-tap – When applicable, to zoom in or out of a web page.

? DID YOU KNOW?

From the Home screen you can tap Settings and then Safari to configure various Safari options, such as the search engine you'd like to use and whether links should open in new pages or in the background.

HOT TIP: When you open Safari it opens to the last page viewed.

Change the search engine

A search engine is what enables you to find things on the Internet. There are several companies that provide search engines, including Google, Yahoo! and Bing. If you like one better than the other, you can opt to use that one when you search in Safari.

1 From the Home screen, tap Settings.

2 Tap Safari. Note that a 'back' button becomes available.

3 Tap Search Engine.

4 Tap the desired option.

5 Tap Safari and then Settings to return to the main Settings screen.

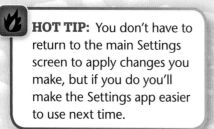

HOT TIP: You don't have to return to the main Settings screen to apply changes you make, but if you do you'll make the Settings app easier to use next time.

? DID YOU KNOW?
If you don't like Safari in general, you can get another web browser from the App Store. (The App Store is detailed in Chapter 10.) Chrome and Opera Mini Web are quite popular.

Use private browsing

As you surf the Internet with Safari, certain aspects of your session are saved. Websites you visit are saved to the History list, available from the Bookmarks icon. Cookies and data are saved too. If you don't want Safari to keep this information, you must enable Private Browsing.

1 From the Home screen, tap Settings.

2 Tap Safari.

3 Move the slider for Private Browsing from Off to On.

4 When prompted, choose Close All to close existing tabs. This enables you to start a completely new Safari session.

HOT TIP: If other people (including children or spouses) use your iPhone and you don't want them to know what websites you've visited, enable Private Browsing and close all Safari windows when you're finished with them.

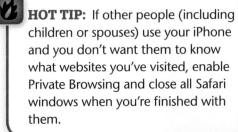

WHAT DOES THIS MEAN?

Cookies: Small bits of information that websites place on your iPhone that allow websites to remember you and your preferences and passwords, among other things.

Clear history, data and cookies

If you don't want to opt for Private Browsing all of the time, but sometimes want to delete the items in the History list and any data that Safari has saved, you do so in Settings.

1 From the Home screen, tap Settings.

2 Tap Safari.

3 Tap Clear History, and Clear History again to verify.

4 Repeat to clear Cookies and Data.

HOT TIP: To access History in Safari, tap the Bookmarks icon and tap History (you may have to tap an applicable 'back' button to get there.

DID YOU KNOW?
You can also clear your History list from the list itself. Tap Bookmarks, History, then Clear.

5 Communicate with Mail

Introduction

Your iPhone comes with the Mail app, which you use to send and receive email. Mail is integrated and works with other apps on your iPhone. For instance, you can tell Siri to write an email for you; you can initiate an email, complete with pictures attached, via the Photos app; you can email invitations to events you create in the Calendar app; you can email a location from Maps; and much more.

Mail can be used on its own too. From Mail you can compose, read, reply to and forward email, open attachments, view photos included with an email and use gestures to manage the mail you acquire. You can also add photos and videos when composing email, pull down to refresh your mailboxes, and create different signatures for each of your configured accounts. To get started, though, you must tell Mail about the email accounts you want to use.

Explore and enable your iCloud account

If you don't have an email account, you can use an iCloud account. You'll need to enable this in Settings first, and then do some exploring to learn a little about the account, but once that's done you can open Mail and begin using the account to send and receive email.

1 From the Home screen, tap Settings.

2 Tap iCloud. Complete any prompts as applicable.

3 Move the slider for Mail from Off to On, if applicable. Complete any prompts as applicable.

HOT TIP: Even if you have other email accounts, you may still want to enable Mail for iCloud. Email you send and receive through the account are stored 'in the cloud' and can be synced with other iDevices you own.

WHAT DOES THIS MEAN?

The cloud or iCloud: Terms used to denote that data created in an app is stored on the Internet. This means that the data stored there can be synced to and be made available from other iDevices you own, as well as computers that offer Internet access. It's like a remote hard drive for your iPhone.

4 Just above Mail, tap the Account name.

5 Scroll down to Advanced, and next to Mail, note your iCloud account.

Advanced	
Mail	joliballew@me.com >

6 Tap Done.

7 Tap the Home button to access the Home screen, and then tap Mail.

8 Note that your new iCloud account is available. Tap iCloud under All Inboxes, if applicable, to access your iCloud email.

```
 ..... AT&T 🤍        1:24 PM          ▭)

                 Mailboxes      Edit

  Inboxes

     📭  All Inboxes          1   >

     ⭐  VIP                      >

     📭  iCloud                   >
```

▶ **SEE ALSO:** Chapter 1, the sections entitled Understand iCloud, and Enable or disable iCloud.

🔥 **HOT TIP:** If and when you configure other email accounts to use in Mail, you'll see those accounts listed under iCloud from the Mailboxes screen.

❓ **DID YOU KNOW?**
You can add your important contacts to the VIP list to group email from those contacts and have easy access to them.

Set up a web-based account

If you have another web-based email account you use, such as one you may have obtained from Gmail, Yahoo!, AOL and the like, you can configure it easily for use in Mail.

 From the Home screen, tap Settings.

 Tap Mail, Contacts, Calendars.

 Tap Add Account.

4 Choose the type of account to add. (Scroll to see more, if necessary. If you don't see your account type, you'll have to tap Other.)

5 Fill out the required information and tap Next.

6 As applicable, configure additional options and tap Save.

Set up a POP3 or SMTP account

If you have an email account from an Internet service provider (ISP), such as Zen or BT, you'll have to select Other during the set-up process that was detailed in the previous section. Then you will have to input the information provided to you by the ISP. What is required differs for each ISP.

1 From the Home screen, tap Settings.

2 Tap Mail, Contacts, Calendars.

3 Tap Add Account, scroll down in the results and then tap Other.

4 Tap Add Mail Account.

Add Account...	**Other**
Mail	
Add Mail Account	>

5 Type the desired information, tap Next, and continue until all information has been input.

6 Tap Save.

! ALERT: Configuring these kinds of accounts can be difficult. If you have problems, contact your ISP and ask them to walk you through it.

? DID YOU KNOW?
ISPs store incoming email on their own email servers, which is why you have to type the name of those servers if your iPhone can't find them on its own.

Choose a default account

If you've configured more than one email account in Mail, you should choose which account will be the default. The default account will be used when you send an email from another app, and when no specific 'Inbox' is selected in Mail when you opt to compose.

1 From the Home screen, tap Settings.

2 Tap Mail, Contacts, Calendars.

3 Scroll down and tap Default Account.

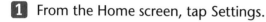

Increase Quote Level	On >
Signature Sent from my iPhone	>
Default Account	iCloud >

Messages created outside of Mail will be sent from the default account.

4 Tap the desired account.

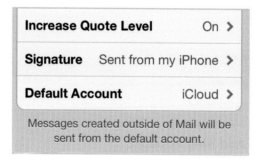

Mail... **Default Account**	
iCloud	
Gmail	✓
Yahoo!	
Hotmail	

HOT TIP: When in Settings, tap the appropriate 'back' button(s) to return to the main Settings screen before closing the app. It'll be easier to use next time.

HOT TIP: Take a look at all of the other options that are available from the screen that offers Default Account. Just above Default Account is the option to change the email signature, for instance.

Understand the Mail interface hierarchy

The Mail interface offers, among other things, a Compose button, available on every Mail screen. Additionally, there is a type of hierarchy involved, as there is with other apps, so there are various 'back' buttons to explore as they become available.

1 The main Mail page does not have a 'back' button. It's the default landing page for Mail.

2 The two sections available from the landing page, Inboxes and Accounts, offer access to your email. Inboxes offers a way to access new mail only; Accounts offers access to the Inbox and other folders for an account such as Trash, Sent Mail or Drafts.

DID YOU KNOW?

From the Mailboxes page, tap VIP and add your most important contacts. Then, you can easily access mail just from them by tapping VIP any time. You can even configure custom alerts!

- If you tap All Inboxes or a single Inbox, you'll have access to new mail in that Inbox (or all of them). A 'back' button appears.

- If you tap any item under Accounts, the available folders for the account become available (as does a 'back' button).

 HOT TIP: When you tap any Inbox, Mail will check for new email.

HOT TIP: Most of the time you'll be in All Inboxes.

Compose an email the old-fashioned way

You can tap the Compose button on Mail's landing page and while in All Inboxes to start a new email that will be sent from the default Mail account. To use a different account, tap the desired account's Inbox before tapping Compose, or make the change by tapping the From line during the composition process.

1 To start a new email, tap the Compose button.

2 Type the recipient's email address in the To line, or, tap the + sign and choose the recipient from the Contacts list. If the email appears as you type, click it.

3 Tap in the Subject line and type your subject.

4 Tap in the body and type your message.

5 Tap Send.

? **DID YOU KNOW?**
To change which account to send an email-in-progress from, in the New Message window, tap the CC, BCC, From line. Tap the From line and choose the desired account from which to send.

Compose an email with dictation

It's no longer necessary to type emails, provided you are connected to the Internet when you compose them. You can dictate them.

1 Tap the Compose button.

2 Tap the microphone on the keyboard and say the name of the person you'd like to send the email to. Tap Done.

3 Tap the desired recipient from the resulting list.

4 Tap inside the Subject line.

5 Tap the microphone button on the keyboard and say the subject. (Remember to say any punctuation as well.) Tap Done.

6 Tap inside the body and repeat.

7 Tap Send.

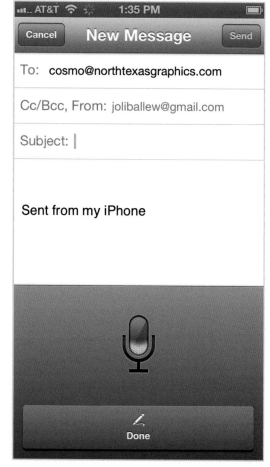

HOT TIP: If what you see on the screen isn't what you dictated, tap and hold to place the cursor where the mistake is, and correct it using the keyboard.

HOT TIP: You must say the punctuation you want to be typed. For instance, 'Do you want to go to lunch question mark.'

Compose an email with Siri

You can tell Siri you want to send an email, and then tell him to whom to send it and what it should say. Return to the Home screen now, to get the full Siri experience.

1 Press and hold the Home button. When the purple microphone appears, say, 'Siri, send an email'.

2 State the name of a contact. If Siri can't deduce which contact you mean, he'll offer options. Pick one if applicable.

```
..ıl... AT&T 📶          12:44 PM              ▭

   Which 'Cosmo'?

   North Texas Graphics (Co...

   Mary Cosmo

   Iris Cosmo

   Mary Anne Cosmo

   North Texas texas Graphi...



              🎤
```

HOT TIP: You don't have to say, 'Siri, send an email'. You can shorten it and say, 'Send an email to <contact>'.

3 State the subject when prompted.

4 State what the email should say, when prompted.

5 Tap Send or tell Siri it's okay to send it.

Read, reply to and/or forward email

As you receive email, you'll want to read it and perhaps send a reply or perform some other task.

1 Locate and then tap an email to read, perhaps from All Inboxes.

2 To respond to the email, tap the left-facing arrow at the bottom of the screen.

- Tap Reply, Reply All (only available when the email was sent to multiple recipients), or Forward.

> **Reply**
>
> **Forward**
>
> **Print**
>
> **Cancel**

- Complete the email as desired and tap Send.

3 To delete an email, tap the Trash icon. It's the middle icon at the bottom of the screen.

 HOT TIP: Pull down from the top when in any Inbox to check for new email (to refresh the list).

HOT TIP: While in a list of emails in any Inbox, tap Edit. You can then select multiple emails and delete them all at once.

? DID YOU KNOW?

The icon to the left of the Trash icon is the Move icon. You may be able to tap Move and choose a folder to move the open email to, but this depends on the email addresses you use and how you've configured them.

Add a photo to an email

You can attach a photo to an email-in-progress. Just double-tap inside the body of the message, tap the right arrow, and tap Insert Photo or Video. However, you can select up to five photos at once from the Photos app and opt to share them via email instead. Sometimes, this is more convenient.

1 From the Home screen, tap Photos.

2 Tap any 'back' buttons as required to get to the Photos landing page. Make sure Albums is selected.

SEE ALSO: The section entitled Explore the Photos app, in Chapter 7.

HOT TIP: Landing pages for apps don't have a 'back' button.

3 Tap the folder that contains the photo(s) to email. You may choose Camera Roll, for instance.

4 Tap the Edit button.

5 Tap up to five photos to send via email.

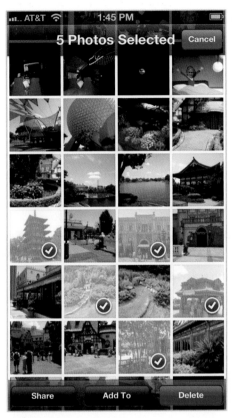

6 Tap Share (shown), then Mail (not shown).

7 Complete the email as desired; tap Send.

8 Choose a photo size.

HOT TIP: When emailing photos when you aren't connected to Wi-Fi, choose a smaller photo size when sending. If you're connected to Wi-Fi you can choose a larger size without having to worry about your data limits.

Open an attachment

When you receive photos in an email, you don't have to open them. They are embedded in the email. (You can tap and hold any photo to save it to your iPhone though.) However, other types of attachments can't be embedded, such as Word documents, spreadsheets, videos and so on.

1 Tap any email that contains an attachment.

2 Scroll down if necessary to locate the attachment. Tap it to download it.

? **DID YOU KNOW?**

An email that contains an attachment will have a paperclip on it.

3 Tap the downloaded icon to open the attachment, and tap Message when you've finished viewing it.

Use gestures to manage email

As with other apps, you can use gestures such as swiping up or down to access the parts of an email that don't show on the screen. There are other gestures to try though.

1 Tap any image once to save it, or all of the images included in the email, to your iPhone.

2 While in any Inbox, tap Edit and then tap once on each email to delete. Tap Delete or Archive.

3 While in any Inbox, swipe from left to right to access the option to delete the email. (You might see Delete or Archive, for example.)

Joli Ballew
Testing!
● Thanks! Joli Ballew, MCT, MCSE, MCTS, MVP, MCDST IT Professor and Microsoft Academic IT Coor...

Delete

4 Pinch in or out to zoom in and out on an email.

5 Double-tap any text and then drag from the blue handles to copy, select or define the selected word or text.

Learn hands-on with free workshops.
Attend f
Apple R

Copy | Select All | Define

the features of your ne● i●●one —
including built-in apps, iCloud, and
iOS 6.
Find an Apple Retail Store ▸

? DID YOU KNOW?
You can also double-tap an image to copy it.

Personalise Mail

You'll find personalisation options in the Settings app, under Mail, Contacts, Calendar. You scroll down to view them. Here are a few to try out.

..... AT&T 🛜	2:08 PM	🔋

◁ Settings	**Mail, Contacts, Calen...**

Mail

1	Show	50 Recent Messages ❯
2	Preview	3 Lines ❯
	Show To/Cc Label	⬜ OFF
	Ask Before Deleting	⬜ OFF
	Load Remote Images	ON ⬜
3	Organize By Thread	⬜ OFF

Always Bcc Myself	⬜ OFF
Increase Quote Level	On ❯
Signature	Sent from my iPhone ❯
Default Account	Gmail ❯

1 Show – To show up to 1,000 recent messages in Mail.

2 Preview – To show how many lines should appear in an Inbox for the email (prior to opening it).

3 Organize By Thread – To stop grouping emails together if they contain the same subject line (or to enable this feature).

HOT TIP: If you need a copy of all of the email you send from your iPhone, enable Always Bcc Myself.

HOT TIP: If you want Mail to ask you to confirm you really want to delete an email when you tap Delete, enable Ask Before Deleting.

Change your signature

The signature *Sent from my iPhone* is added to all email you send. You can remove this and not use any signature, or you can replace the signature with something else.

1 From the Home screen, tap Settings.

2 Tap Mail, Contacts, Calendars.

3 Tap Signature.

4 Opt to apply the signature to all accounts or for only a specific account.

5 Tap Sent from my iPhone, and then type a new signature.

HOT TIP: You may want to keep *Sent from my iPhone* as the signature so people know you're away from the office when you send them an email, or you may want to remove it so people don't know you're away from the office!

6 Read books and magazines

Introduction

Even though the iPhone's screen is small, you can still read digital books on it using the iBooks app. You can read magazines and newspapers too, if you subscribe to their compatible, electronic versions, using the Newsstand app. Additionally, you can access media from universities, including entire courses, using the iTunes U app.

There are media available from places other than the Apple Store though. You may be familiar with Amazon, and Amazon offers an app called Kindle that you can use to read electronic books you buy there. You find and install these apps in the App Store (detailed in Chapter 10), but you'll get a little preview of them here if you're interested).

You'll need to be connected to the Internet to shop for and download books, media and magazines from any source, but once they are downloaded to and stored on your iPhone you generally don't have to be connected to read them.

Install iBooks

iBooks is the app you use to read books you acquire from Apple's iBookstore. It also offers quick access to the store for purchasing books. Your iPhone does not come pre-installed with iBooks, so you'll have to obtain it.

1 From the Home screen, tap App Store. (If this is your first visit to the store, you may be prompted to obtain iBooks and other missing apps without having to search for them.)

2 Tap the Search icon.

3 Tap inside the Search window and type iBooks.

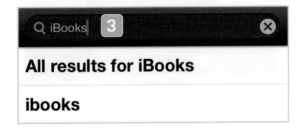

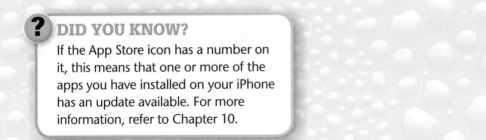

? DID YOU KNOW?

If the App Store icon has a number on it, this means that one or more of the apps you have installed on your iPhone has an update available. For more information, refer to Chapter 10.

4 Tap iBooks in the results.

5 Tap Free next to iBooks (if it's already installed you'll see Open, as shown here).

6 Tap Install App, type your password and tap OK.

7 Tap the Home button to exit the App Store.

? DID YOU KNOW?
It only takes a few seconds for an app to install, but you must be connected to the Internet. A connection via Wi-Fi is best.

HOT TIP: The new app will download and its icon will appear on one of your Home screens.

Explore the iBookstore

The iBookstore is organised by tabs. You tap the tabs to access the available books in various ways. One of the options is Charts, for instance, where you can view the current Top Paid and Top Free books. Browse is an option too, where you can browse by author, again by Top Paid and Top Free. You'll use Search to look for something specific, perhaps by title or author, when necessary.

1 Tap iBooks. It is probably on a secondary Home screen.

2 Once open and you have access to the Bookshelf, tap Store.

 HOT TIP: The iBookstore has a hierarchy like other apps you've already explored. For instance, if you tap a book to learn more about it, a new 'back' button appears. You tap it to return to the page you were previously viewing.

3 Tap each of the available tabs at the bottom of the screen. You could tap Charts and then tap NY Times, for instance.

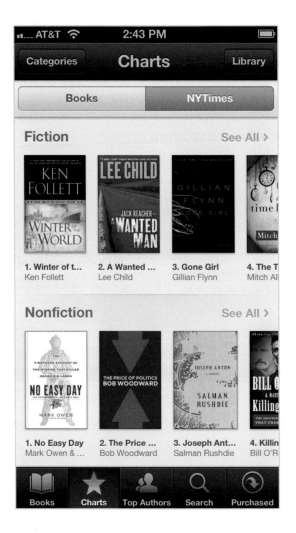

? DID YOU KNOW?

Several of the tabs offer a Categories button. Tap it to cull the results by category, such as Humor, Mysteries & Thrillers, Romance, and so on. (If you don't want to select a category, click Cancel.)

Preview a book

You can preview any book in the iBookstore. You only need to locate the book to sample and tap the Get Sample button.

1 Open iBooks and, if required, tap Store. You may already be in the store.

2 Locate a book to preview and tap its title.

3 From the resulting Details page, tap Sample. (You can also read reviews here and view related titles.)

4 If required, type your password and then tap OK.

5 Note the new title on the Bookshelf.

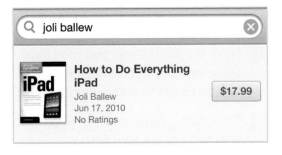

▶ **SEE ALSO:** The section Read a book, later in this chapter.

? DID YOU KNOW?
You can remove any sample book from your Bookshelf by tapping Edit, tapping the book to remove and then tapping Delete.

Buy a book or obtain a free one

If you'd like to acquire a full book and not just a sample of one, you can buy one or obtain one that's free. Any book you purchase (or obtain) on your iPhone can also be read on your other iDevices, including iPads. You must be connected to the Internet to access the store and download books.

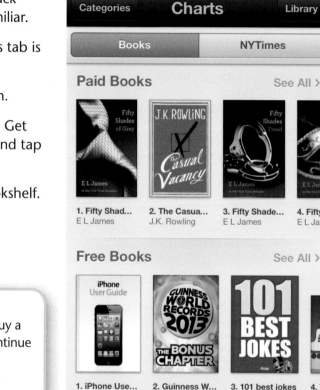

1. Enter the iBookstore. You may have to tap a new tab or an available 'back' button to get to somewhere familiar.

2. Tap Charts, verify that the Books tab is selected. Locate Free Books.

3. Tap the book you'd like to obtain.

4. Tap Free (or the listed price), tap Get Book, and type your password and tap OK if prompted.

5. Note the new book on your Bookshelf.

 **DID YOU KNOW?**

Once you type your password to buy a book or get a free one, you can continue to shop for a while without having to input it again. Thus, if you aren't prompted for your password, it's because you're still in the shopping-without-entering-your-password-again time window.

 **DID YOU KNOW?**

You'll re-enter the store in the same place as you left it last. So if you left the store while on the Details page of a specific book, that's where you'll be when you re-enter the store later.

HOT TIP: If a book has Download beside it, you've already obtained it but it is not currently on your iPhone. Tap Download to put the book on your iPhone.

Read a book

With a book, books or sample books available on your Bookshelf, you can now read one. Once you've opened a book you'll have access to various controls and can flick left to right and right to left to move among the pages.

1 Open iBooks. If you see anything other than the Bookshelf, tap the appropriate 'back' button. You may have to tap library.

2 From the Bookshelf, tap the book to read.

3 Flick left and right to move among the pages. You can also tap the left or right side of the pages.

4 Turn the iPhone 90 degrees to view the book in landscape mode.

5 If you don't see the controls shown here, tap the screen once in the middle.

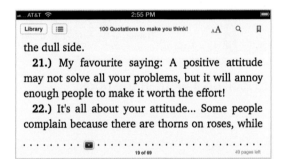

 DID YOU KNOW?
To leave a book and return to the Bookshelf, tap Library. If you don't see the Library option, tap the middle of the screen once.

HOT TIP: Although you can bookmark pages, you don't have to. A book will open where you left off every time.

Explore iBook features

There are five features to explore while reading a book. They are Contents, Fonts, Search, Bookmark and the slider that runs across the bottom of the screen.

1 Contents – Tap to access the table of contents, bookmarks you've created and notes you've written. Resume becomes an option when you do.

2 Fonts – Tap to change the font size, the font or to apply a theme such as Sepia or Night. Note the Brightness slider here too.

3 Search – Tap Search to look up a word in the book.

4 Bookmark – Tap to set a bookmark for the page. You can access your bookmarks from Contents.

5 Slider – Drag the slider to move around quickly in a book. You saw this slider in the previous section. It appears at the bottom of the screen.

? DID YOU KNOW?
You can tap Library to return to the Bookshelf while reading a book.

🔥 HOT TIP: You can tap and hold on text to access additional options. The options include the ability to highlight the text, make a note about it, and more.

Sort books

The Books button on the Bookshelf enables you to sort your print media. There are two kinds of media available; one is the books you are already familiar with (common digital books), the other is PDF files. A PDF is another option for sharing print media online, but is less common than other digital book options.

1 Tap Books from the Bookshelf.

2 Tap PDFs to view any PDFs you've acquired.

3 Tap PDFs and then Books to return to the Books screen.

4 Tap Books again. Tap New.

.ıll AT&T 🛜   1:14 PM   ▭)

Collections | Done |

| Books | ✓ |

| PDFs |

≈

| **New** | Edit |

5 Type the name of a new collection, perhaps Travel, Pets, Gardening, Mysteries, or Nonfiction.

6 Tap Done. Tap Done again.

7 You can now tap Edit on the Bookshelf, tap a book and tap Move to move the selected book into the new collection.

HOT TIP: You don't have to group books if you don't want to. You can tap Edit, select the books you've read and then tap Delete to remove them from the Bookshelf. (You can download them again from the Purchased tab of iBooks if you ever want to.)

? DID YOU KNOW?
Electronic books don't use very much of your iPhone's storage space, so it's okay to keep lots of books on your iPhone.

Explore the Kindle app

If you purchase electronic books from Amazon, you'll quickly discover you can't read them in iBooks. To read books from Amazon, you must acquire the Kindle app from the App Store. Once installed, the Kindle app works similarly to iBooks.

1 Tap the Kindle icon to open the Kindle app.

2 Locate the book to read, and tap it. (It may have to download first.)

3 Flick left and right to move among the pages.

4 Tap once to access the Kindle controls.

Kindle

.ıl. AT&T 🔊   2:58 PM   ▬

| Home | **Alice's Adventur...** | 🔖 |

time to hear it say, as it turned a corner, 'Oh my ears and whiskers, how late it's getting!' She was close behind it when she turned the corner, but the Rabbit was no longer to be seen: she found herself in a long, low hall, which was lit up by a row of lamps hanging from the roof.

There were doors all round the hall, but they were all locked; and when Alice had been all the way down one side and up the other, trying every door, she walked

Aa   📖   🔍   ↻

4% · Page 5 of 124 · Loc 40 of 1125

! **ALERT:** You can't read books you buy from Amazon in iBooks, nor can you read books you buy from the iBookstore in Kindle.

🔥 **HOT TIP:** The Kindle app has a Fonts button, a Search icon and other features similar to iBooks.

Explore Newsstand

146

You use the Newsstand app to access and download additional apps, which are stored inside Newsstand. The apps you acquire are created by the publishers of the available magazines and newspapers. You then use these apps to make magazine and newspaper purchases, to subscribe to publications and to read the media you purchase. At present, all of the apps you acquire here are free. You pay only when you want to make a purchase.

1. Tap Newsstand, and tap Store.

2. Explore the options and locate a magazine or newspaper you'd like to subscribe to. Consider the Daily; its content may be free.

3. Tap Free and then tap Install App. (If you've previously obtained it on another device, tap Install instead.) Input your password and tap OK.

4. Tap Open. Opt to allow or disallow the app to send messages to your iPhone.

5. Tap the Home button to access the Newsstand app again.

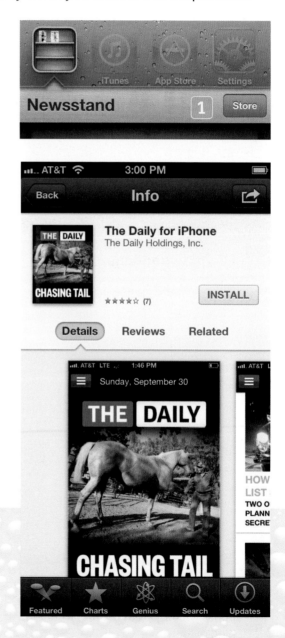

ALERT: If you get lost in Newsstand and can't find Newsstand material (and instead see apps, books and the like), tap the Home button on your iPhone and tap Store again. It'll reopen in Newsstand.

ALERT: Apps you acquire in Newsstand aren't all the same. You'll have to learn how to use the apps you acquire on your own, but generally it's intuitive.

Read a magazine

You read magazines using the app that you downloaded to acquire it. How you use an app differs from one app to another, so you'll need to explore each one independently.

1. Tap Newsstand and tap the desired app on the bookshelf. (If you're in the Newsstand store, press the Home button on your iPhone.)

2. If you haven't made a purchase, you may have to if you want to view media. (Some apps offer free media, but not many.)

3. Use the various controls to move around in the app.

ALERT: Be careful when you subscribe to magazines and newspapers. The subscription will likely renew automatically every year if you don't take precautions to cancel it.

HOT TIP: If you have more apps in the Newsstand than you can view at once, scroll to access them.

Explore iTunes U

iTunes U (iTunes University) is an app similar to iBooks. Like iBooks, you have to get it from the App Store before you can use it. From the iTunes U app you can easily access iTunes U media, which includes, among other things, access to courses from colleges and universities all over the world. Some of these courses are text or audio only, but many are videos.

1 Tap the iTunes U app. (You can get this app from the App Store.)

2 Tap Catalog. View the various tabs across the bottom.

3 Locate a course to subscribe to; tap Subscribe. Complete the checkout process as required.

4 If applicable, tap Library to access your media.

5 Tap the downloaded media. If it is a video lecture, use the controls to manage video playback.

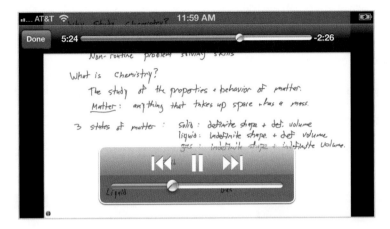

 DID YOU KNOW?
You read iTunes U media by tapping and scrolling. Many courses are text only.

HOT TIP: While reviewing a course, tap the Materials tab to access documents that go with the lecture.

Configure app settings

Most apps offer some options for personalising them. You access an app's options from the Settings app on the Home screen. If you don't see options here, you may be able to configure options from inside the app itself.

1 From the Home screen, tap Settings.

2 Verify that you are at the landing page and that there is no 'back' button.

3 Scroll down to locate the app to configure. Here, iBooks and iTunes U are shown.

4 Tap to view the configuration and personalisation options, and configure them as desired.

Settings

iTunes & App Stores	>
Music	>
Videos	>
Photos & Camera	>
iBooks	>
Newsstand	>
Podcasts	>
iTunes U	>

AT&T 3:09 PM

Settings **iBooks**

iBooks 2.2 (931)

Full Justification	ON
Auto-hyphenation	ON
Tap Left Margin	Previous Page >
Sync Bookmarks	ON
Sync Collections	ON
Online Audio & Video	OFF
Acknowledgements	>

Copyright © 2012 Apple Inc. All rights reserved.

HOT TIP: To move forward one page in iBooks using a tap from your left hand or right, change Tap Left Margin to Next Page.

WHAT DOES THIS MEAN?

Sync: When you **sync bookmarks**, **collections**, and other data, you can access that information from other iDevices.

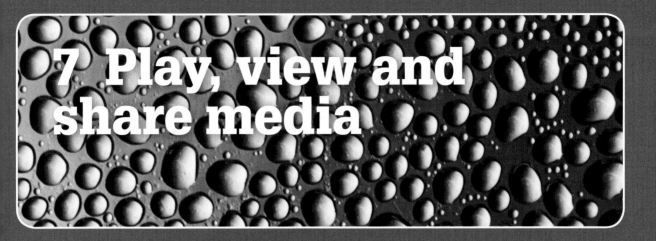

7 Play, view and share media

Introduction

Media is a broad term that is used to represent a lot of different types of data. The media you'll explore in this chapter include music, audiobooks, pictures and video. You can do more than play and view media though; you can share it too. You can let others view your photos, watch a video with a friend, and even 'stream' your personal music over a home network.

Explore the Music app

The Music app, available from the Home screen (on the Dock) is similar to other apps you've explored. It has a hierarchical order (complete with 'back' buttons that appear as you navigate through it), tabs to assist in navigation, and access to the iTunes Store.

Open the Music app by tapping it once, and then explore these tabs:

1 Genius – To access Genius recommendations that are based on your current music library.

2 Playlists – To view existing playlists, create a new playlist or create a Genius Playlist.

3 Artists – To view an alphabetical list of the artists in your music library.

WHAT DOES THIS MEAN?

Genius Playlist: A playlist created for you, automatically, based on a single song you pick from your music library.

4 Songs – To view songs in your library alphabetically.

5 Albums – To view songs in your library by album.

6 More – To access other types of media, including audiobooks, and to sort music in other ways.

AT&T	3:26 PM	
Edit	**More**	Now Playing
🎵 **Albums**		>
📖 **Audiobooks**		>
👥 **Compilations**		>
🎼 **Composers**		>
🎸 **Genres**		>

6

Genius	Playlists	Artists	Songs	More

HOT TIP: If you don't see any music on your iPhone but you have music on the computer you sync it with, connect the two, choose your iPhone in the left pane of iTunes, click the Music tab and choose some songs to sync.

SEE ALSO: Refer to Chapter 10 to learn how to purchase music from the iTunes Store.

Play a song

To play a song you need only to navigate to it and tap it once. If the song is in any kind of list, perhaps part of an album or playlist, the next song in the list will play after it finishes.

1 Locate any song in the Music app and tap it.

2 Use the controls to start the song over, pause or skip to the next song.

3 Tap the Track List icon to view the songs in the list; tap the icon again (now a thumbnail of the album art) to return to Album Art view.

4 Tap applicable 'back' buttons to move back a page in the hierarchy.

5 Tap Now Playing to access the album page.

DID YOU KNOW?

By default, even when the screen is dark and/or the phone locked, you can control the volume of the music using the volume buttons on the outside of the phone.

WHAT DOES THIS MEAN?

Shuffle: To play the songs in a list in random order. The Shuffle icon looks like two criss-crossing arrows.

Create a playlist

A playlist is a group of songs, such as songs that appear on an album. You can create your own playlists, name them, and add songs that you choose, to group music together according to your preferences. Once saved, the playlists will appear under the Playlists tab.

1 Open the Music app and tap the Playlists tab.

2 Tap Add Playlist.

3 Type a name for the playlist and tap Save.

? DID YOU KNOW?

If you create a playlist on your iPhone and then sync it with your computer, the playlist will be synced if syncing is set up as such.

4 Tap each song to add and tap Done.

5 Tap Playlists to return to the previous page in the hierarchy.

 HOT TIP: A playlist only contains names of songs; the actual music isn't moved anywhere or copied to a new location, and thus, it's okay to create as many playlists as you like without worrying about storage issues.

Listen to an audiobook

If you've purchased audiobooks, you can listen to them with the Music app, provided they are of a compatible file format. (Companies who produce audiobooks, such as Audible, offer apps for listening to audiobooks if they won't play in the Music app.)

1 In the Music app, tap More then tap Audiobooks.

2 If you see the audiobook, tap it; if you see a folder instead, tap it.

3 Tap the title of any audiobook (or part of an audiobook) to play it.

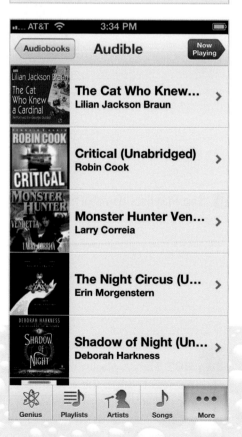

4 Use the controls to manage the audiobook and the back button to navigate the app.

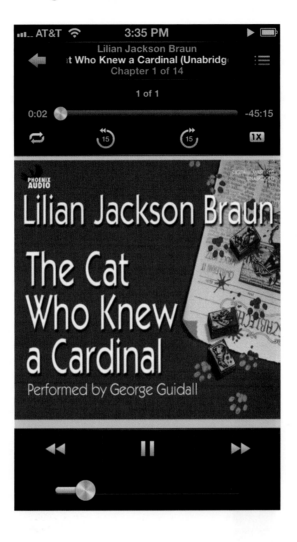

🔥 **HOT TIP:** Audiobooks are often split into sections to make the download faster. You may see folders that represent the sections.

⚠️ **ALERT:** Audiobook files can be quite large, so you should remove audiobooks you've already listened to. One way to do this is by connecting your iPhone to your computer and choosing what to sync (and what not to).

Explore the Photos app

When you take pictures with your iPhone or sync photos from your computer (or acquire them in some other way, perhaps saving them from an email), they appear in the Photos app. The Photos app is on the Home screen. This app is hierarchical like other apps, contains folders for organising the photos you keep, and has a landing page that you can recognise easily (the landing page does not have a 'back' button).

1 Tap Photos on the Home screen and tap any applicable 'back' buttons until you are on the Photos landing page with Albums selected at the bottom.

.ıl... AT&T 🛜	**3:36 PM**	▭
+	**Albums**	**Edit**
	Camera Roll (331)	>
	Photo Library (860)	>
	Allison Favorites (22)	>
	Friends (31)	>
	Houses (298)	>
	Me, Jennifer, Mom,... (190)	>
	My Favorites (60)	>
	Pets (144)	>
1 Albums	Photo Stream	Places

ALERT: What you see on your iPhone will differ from what's shown here. You may not have additional folders, for example.

2 Tap Camera Roll, scroll to view the photos and then tap Photo Stream and Places, as applicable.

3 As you explore the app, tap any folder that you know contains pictures.

4 Tap any photo to view it in full screen mode.

5 Tap the screen and tap the applicable back buttons to return to the landing page.

? DID YOU KNOW?

While viewing a single photo in *full screen mode*, you have access to a Back button, Edit button, Share button and Play button. You'll learn about these later in this chapter. You may also see a Trash icon. You can use this to delete a photo.

? DID YOU KNOW?

While in any *folder* you have access to an Edit button that enables you to select photos and then perform actions on them as a group. Share is one option, and from there you can opt to mail, message, copy, and more.

Play a slideshow

You can play a slideshow of photos in a folder simply by navigating to a picture in the folder and tapping the Play button. The slideshow will play until you tap the screen again.

1 From the Photos landing page, select any folder.

2 Tap any picture in the folder, and then tap the Play button. (If you don't see this button, tap the screen once.)

3 If desired, tap to choose a transition and select a song to play in the background.

4 Tap Start Slideshow.

? DID YOU KNOW?

A slideshow will continue to play until you stop it; this means that when the slideshow reaches the last picture in a folder it will start again at the beginning.

WHAT DOES THIS MEAN?

Transition: How one picture 'moves' or 'changes' into another. Try Ripple to see a cool transition effect.

Share a photo while in full screen mode

You can share a single photo you've opened in full screen mode in many ways. You can email it, send it in a message, assign it to a contact, use it as wallpaper, send it in a tweet, and print it.

1 Locate a photo you want to share, and tap it so that it opens in full screen mode.

2 Tap the screen if you can't see the Share button, and then tap it.

3 Tap the desired option. What happens after this depends on which option you've selected.

WHAT DOES THIS MEAN?

iMessage: A message you send with the Messages app (see Chapter 9).

⚠ **ALERT:** You can't print a photo using just any printer. It has to be a printer specifically created for use with iDevices.

Edit a photo and save changes

Yes, you can lightly edit photos using your iPhone! Editing options include rotating the image, applying auto enhancements, fixing red-eye and cropping the image.

1 Locate any photo to edit and tap it. It should be in full screen mode.

2 Tap Edit.

3 Tap the Rotate button to rotate the image if applicable.

4 Tap the Auto Enhance button to apply automatic enhancements.

5 Tap the Red-Eye button and then tap to remove red-eye in any subject (if applicable). Tap Apply.

6 Tap the Crop button and drag the rectangle to the desired part of the image.

7 Tap Crop.

8 Tap Save and then tap Save to Camera Roll.

HOT TIP: To access the edited image, open the Camera Roll folder.

? DID YOU KNOW?

When you view a photo in full screen mode that is stored in the Camera Roll or the Photo Stream folder, a Trash button appears. You can use this to delete a photo. You will not be able to delete photos from other folders (you have to do this by syncing with your computer).

Assign a photo to a contact or use as wallpaper

You saw earlier that Assign to Contact and Use as Wallpaper were two options from the Share button when viewing a picture in full screen mode. Making this happen is simple.

1 To apply a photo to a contact:
- Locate a photo to use for a contact and tap the Share button.
- Tap Assign to Contact.
- Tap the contact from the resulting list.
- Drag and pinch to move and scale the photo as desired.
- Tap Choose.

2 To use a photo as wallpaper:
- Repeat the steps above except this time choose Use as Wallpaper.
- Tap Set. Tap where to apply the photo.

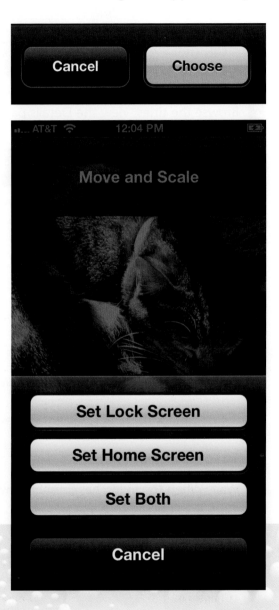

 HOT TIP: When choosing a photo to assign to a contact, use a head shot and scale the image so that it takes up the entire window.

 HOT TIP: When choosing a photo for the Home screen, pick one that isn't too busy or one that has too many lines or colours. It will make seeing the icons for the apps difficult. You can choose just about anything for the Lock screen.

Get a free video from iTunes U

If you want to explore videos, you'll need to acquire one. iTunes U offers lots of free videos if you don't have any. If you have already purchased a movie, TV show or similar media from the iTunes Store, there's no need to do this unless you want to.

1 Open the iTunes U app.

2 Browse the titles, view the Details pages and find an entry that has a video icon beside it.

3 Tap the Download button.

4 Wait. When the video has finished downloading (and shows Downloaded), click the item. It will begin to play.

▶ **SEE ALSO:** Learn how to get the iTunes U app in Chapter 6.

? **DID YOU KNOW?**

The iTunes U app looks and acts like iBooks. There's a bookshelf and your courses appear there; when you tap a title, it opens.

Explore the Videos app

You watch compatible video media using the Videos app. This includes movies, TV shows, video podcasts, music videos and more. You'll see the titles when you open the Videos app.

1 From the Home screen, tap Videos.

2 Tap any title to play it.

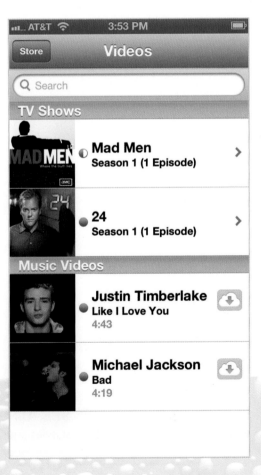

3 Tap to view the controls.

4 Tap Done when finished.

▶ **SEE ALSO:** Learn how to shop for movies and TV shows in Chapter 10.

? DID YOU KNOW?
You can buy music videos from the Store.

 HOT TIP: If you don't see iTunes U content in the Videos app, open the iTunes U app and look for it there.

Explore video controls

The controls available in the Videos app are similar to the controls you're already used to, and much like the controls you'll see in other apps like Music. As with other apps that offer controls, the controls disappear when inactive. Tap the screen to show them.

1 With a video playing, tap the screen once to show the controls.

Note the following controls:

2 Rewind

3 Play/Pause

4 Fast Forward

5 Slider (to move quickly through the video)

6 Volume

7 Full Screen

8 Done

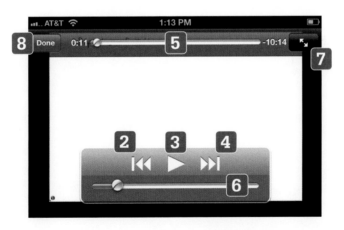

? DID YOU KNOW?
The Videos app has a hierarchy like other apps, and 'back' buttons may appear as you navigate through the app.

🔥 HOT TIP: When you see Get More Episodes in the Videos app, you can tap it to go to the iTunes Store where you can make your purchase.

Set up Home Sharing

If you have a wireless home network and your iPhone can connect to it, and if you have media to share, you can enable Home Sharing. Once enabled on both your computer (via iTunes) and your iPhone (via Settings), you can share media between them. This means, for one thing, that you can access media stored on home computer(s) from your iPhone without actually having to place the media on it.

1 At your computer, open iTunes. The computer should have media you want to share saved to it. Then, in iTunes:

- Click Advanced.
- Click Turn on Home Sharing.
- Follow the prompts to enable this feature.

2 From your iPhone:

- Tap Settings from the Home screen.
- Tap Music or Videos (either will work).
- Under Home Sharing, type the Apple ID and password you used to configure Home Sharing on your computer in step 1.
- Tap Done.

.ıl... AT&T 📶   3:59 PM   🔋

< Settings   **Videos**

Start Playing   Where Left Off >

Closed Captioning   OFF

Home Sharing

Apple ID: joliballew@gmail.com

ALERT: You can only access shared network media when your iPhone is connected to the home network and the computer that contains the media is turned on and awake.

HOT TIP: Apple offers the iTunes Match service for a yearly fee, and with it, you can access your favourite music from virtually anywhere.

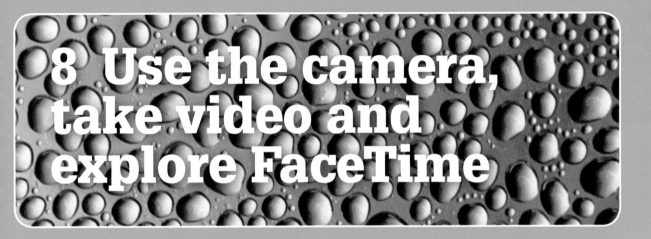

8 Use the camera, take video and explore FaceTime

Introduction

You learned how to watch movies, TV shows, podcasts and the like in the last chapter. Here you'll learn about some of the other video applications available on your iPhone. You'll learn how to take pictures and video with the camera and how to use Photo Stream to save photos to iCloud. After that, you'll learn how to use FaceTime to have a video conversation with your FaceTime contacts.

Take a simple picture

You can take a traditional photo with only a few taps. You first open the Camera app from either the Home screen or the Lock screen, focus, and then tap the shutter icon.

1 Open the Camera app:

- From the Lock screen, tap and drag the camera icon upwards.
- From the Home screen, tap the camera icon.

2 Make sure that the digital camera icon is selected and not the video camera icon.

3 If desired, pinch to zoom in (and then out) on your subject.

4 When you're ready, tap the shutter icon.

HOT TIP: To view the last photo taken quickly, tap the thumbnail in the bottom left corner of the Camera app's screen.

❓ DID YOU KNOW?

Your iPhone has two camera lenses, one on the front and one on the back. If you see yourself instead of what's in front of you, tap the icon in the top right corner to switch lenses.

Focus on your subject

Your iPhone makes some assumptions about what you want to focus on when you frame a shot. You can tap once on the screen to tell your iPhone you want to focus on some other part of the picture. This will cause the camera to refocus and adjust the shot, and should result in a better picture.

1 Point the camera so that there are several available points of focus (perhaps a group of people standing various distances from you).

2 Wait to see what the camera focuses on. You can tell by the rectangle that appears on the screen.

3 To focus on a different part of the picture, tap the desired part.

4 Wait while the camera refocuses, then take your shot.

HOT TIP: Make sure to hold your iPhone steady and to keep your finger or thumb out of the shot!

? DID YOU KNOW?
You can delete pictures you've taken but do not want from the Photos app. Tap Camera Roll, tap the picture to delete and then tap the Trash icon.

Change flash settings

You may have noticed the Auto icon in the top left corner of the Camera app while taking a digital photo. This is where you change the flash settings. The default setting, Auto, will apply the flash only when the app deems necessary. You can set it so that it is on or off.

1 Open the Camera app.

2 Tap Auto.

3 Tap On or Off.

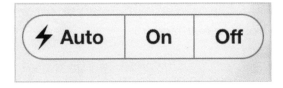

ALERT: If you choose to turn the flash on or off, that setting will remain the default until you change it.

DID YOU KNOW?
Tap Options to show a grid on the screen if you need help framing your shot.

Switch cameras and camera views

Very soon you'll learn how to take video with the video camera. Before you do, you need to know how to switch to the video camera, how to take still photos using HDR (high dynamic range), set up for a panoramic picture, and the limitations that exist for video recording. Additionally, for future reference, you need to know how to switch from the rear- to the front-facing digital camera.

1 Tap to enable high dynamic range, show the grid, and to opt to take a panoramic picture.

2 Tap to switch to the front- or rear-facing camera.

3 Pinch to zoom in or out. You can only zoom when taking still photos.

4 Slide to move from the digital camera to the video camera, and back.

5 Tap to view the last picture or video taken.

 HOT TIP: If you ever need a makeshift flashlight, open the camera and switch to video, then, turn the flash on. (You don't have to record anything.)

WHAT DOES THIS MEAN?

High dynamic range: A high dynamic range (HDR) image combines a series of photographs, each shot at a different exposure. One is underexposed, where everything is darker; another overexposed, where everything is lighter; and one is properly exposed. These images are put together into one shot. If you seem unable to get the shot you want, try this mode.

Enable or disable Photo Stream

Photo Stream is a part of iCloud (see Chapter 1). You can use it to back up your latest 1,000 photos to Apple's Internet servers, and to have access to those photos from any other iDevice you own (that also use Photo Stream). If you use Photo Stream you won't have to worry about losing all of the photos you've taken if something happens to your iPhone.

1 From the Home screen, tap Settings.

2 Tap iCloud.

3 Configure the desired setting for Photo Stream.

ᵐᵗᵗ AT&T 🔋	9:21 AM	🔋
Settings	**iCloud**	
✉ Mail		ON
👤 Contacts		ON
📅 Calendars		ON
☑ Reminders		ON
🧭 Safari		ON
📝 Notes		ON
🎫 Passbook		ON
🌼 Photo Stream	**3**	On >
📄 Documents & Data		On >
🌐 Find My iPhone		ON

Find My iPhone allows you to locate this iPhone on a map and remotely lock or erase it

! ALERT: Photo Stream keeps your most recent photos for 30 days and saves up to 1,000. Once you've reached that threshold, the oldest are replaced with the newest. To keep photos from being inadvertently lost, sync your iPhone to your computer regularly.

? DID YOU KNOW?

If you want to save a picture permanently, and that picture is stored in Photo Stream, open the Photos app, open the Photo Stream folder, tap the Share button and then select the photo (or photos) you want to save permanently to your iPhone. Then tap Save.

Take a video with the camera

Taking a video with the Camera app is quite simple. You simply select the video camera, point and shoot.

1 Open the Camera app and move the slider so that the video camera is selected.

2 Note the options to enable the flash, switch camera lenses, and record.

3 Tap the red Record button.

4 Tap the red Record button to stop recording.

5 To view the video right away, tap the thumbnail in the bottom left corner.

HOT TIP: If you want to email a video, make the recording as short as you can. Video files are quite large and take a long time to deliver.

DID YOU KNOW?
HDR only works with photos, not videos. However, your iPhone records video in 1080P HD, and that will do just fine!

View and share video you've captured

If you've just finished recording a video with the Camera app, you can tap the thumbnail in the bottom left corner to view it. You can also access your video from the Photos app. There, you can play it and share it.

1 Open the Photos app and make sure Albums is selected.

2 Tap Camera Roll.

3 Locate the video to play. It will have a video camera icon on it.

? DID YOU KNOW?

Videos aren't uploaded to Photo Stream, so you'll have to sync your iPhone with your computer to create a backup of the video you shoot.

4 Tap the video and tap Play.

5 When the video finishes, tap the screen to show the controls and tap the Share button.

6 Note the options: Mail, Message, YouTube.

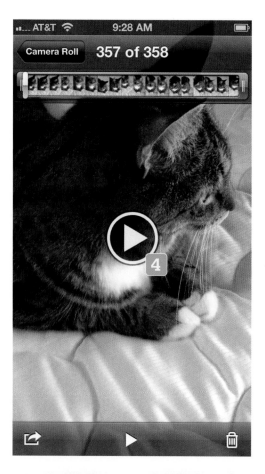

Explore the Photos & Camera settings

There are a few options in the Photos & Camera settings worth exploring. One is Shared Photo Streams. By default this is enabled and allows you to create photo streams to share with others using the Photos app. To access this option and others, tap Settings, and then tap Photos & Settings.

1 Enable My Photo Stream to automatically sync your iPhone photos to other iDevices you own.

2 Enable Shared Photo Streams to create Photo Streams to share in the Photos app. (From Photos, tap the Photo Stream tab and then the + sign.)

3 Configure Slideshow settings.

4 Choose to keep the normal photo as well as the HDR photo when applicable.

```
....ıl AT&T 🔋          10:27 AM              🔋

Settings   Photos & Camera

Photo Stream

My Photo Stream                        ON

Automatically upload new photos and
send them to all of your iCloud devices
       when connected to Wi-Fi.

Shared Photo Streams                   ON

Create photo streams to share with other
people, or subscribe to other people's
       shared photo streams.

Slideshow

Play Each Slide For       3 Seconds  ❯

Repeat                                OFF

Shuffle                               OFF

HDR (High Dynamic Range)
```

? **DID YOU KNOW?** You can post a video you've taken with your iPhone to YouTube from inside the Photos app.

HOT TIP: Try Shared Photo Streams in the Photos app. Tap the Photo Stream tab, click the + sign, create a name for the Photo Stream and then type the email address with whom to share the Photo Stream with. Tap Edit, and then add your photos.

Explore the Video settings

There are three available settings for videos. You can choose how to start a video you've already started viewing, turn on closed captioning when it's available, and configure Home Sharing.

1 Start Playing options let you choose between Where Left Off and From Beginning.

Settings	Videos	
Start Playing	Where Left Off	>
Closed Captioning		ON

Home Sharing

Apple ID: joliballew@gmail.com

2 Closed Captioning options let you show captions where available.

3 Home Sharing lets you share the videos on your iPhone with your own home network.

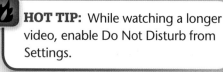 **HOT TIP:** While watching a longer video, enable Do Not Disturb from Settings.

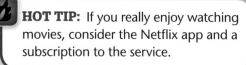 **HOT TIP:** If you really enjoy watching movies, consider the Netflix app and a subscription to the service.

Locate your FaceTime contacts

FaceTime lets you video chat with others who also use iDevices that are FaceTime compatible. You can hold FaceTime conversations over Wi-Fi or a cellular connection. It's best to opt for Wi-Fi any time you can so that you don't go over your monthly data quota.

1 From the Home screen, swipe from left to right to open the Search page.

2 Type Contacts, and tap Contacts from the results.

3 Tap any contact you believe uses an iDevice that includes FaceTime. Compatible contacts will have a video camera icon beside the FaceTime button.

HOT TIP: Ask your friends and family if they have an iPhone that supports FaceTime. If so, look them up in your Contacts list.

HOT TIP: If you see the FaceTime button but do not see a video camera icon beside it, FaceTime can't be used with that contact right now (and perhaps never).

Hold a FaceTime conversation

There are two ways to start a FaceTime conversation: either from a Contact card shown in the previous task, or while in a voice call with a FaceTime contact.

1 From a Contact card:
   - Tap FaceTime.
   - Wait for the recipient to answer.
2 While inside a voice call:
   - Tap FaceTime.
   - Wait for the recipient to accept.
3 To end a FaceTime call, tap End.

HOT TIP: You call tell Siri to initiate a FaceTime video call. Just say, 'Siri, FaceTime <and then state the contact name>'.

DID YOU KNOW? You can hold FaceTime conversations with owners of compatible iPads too.

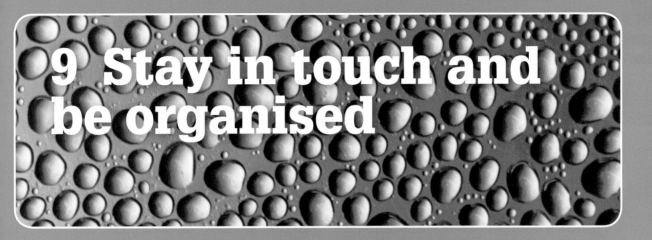

9 Stay in touch and be organised

Introduction

There are several apps on your iPhone that you can use to communicate with others; create, save and share events and appointments; and create and manage to-do lists, notes and reminders. You can use a new app called Passbook to manage boarding passes, store cards, coupons, and so on as well. Most of the apps you'll use to stay organised are iCloud compatible too, which means you can store important data on Apple's Internet servers and then access the information from other places (such as computers and other iDevices). When you use iCloud, any changes you make on one device are synced to other compatible devices automatically (and backed up). You can opt to use iCloud to enhance the effectiveness of the apps introduced here.

Enable the Messages app

You use the Messages app to send *iMessages* to other iPhone, iPad, Mac or iPod touch users (for free over Wi-Fi), and to send regular *text and multimedia messages* to non-iDevice users at regular texting rates. You need to verify the app is enabled from Settings.

1 From the Home screen, tap Settings.

2 Tap Messages.

3 Move the slider for iMessages from Off to On.

4 Opt to use your Apple ID when prompted, type your Apple ID and password and tap Sign In. Tap Next.

5 Configure other options as desired; to use Messages to send texts to non-iPhone users, enable Send as Sms.

Settings

✉	Mail, Contacts, Calendars	>
▭	Notes	>
▤	Reminders	>
📞	Phone	>
💬	Messages **2**	>
◉	FaceTime	>

····· AT&T 🛜 10:52 AM ▬▬

Settings **Messages**

iMessage   **ON**

iMessages can be sent between iPhone, iPad, iPod touch, and Mac.
Learn More

Send Read Receipts   **OFF**

Allow others to be notified when you have read their messages.

Send as SMS **5** **ON**

Send as SMS when iMessage is unavailable. Carrier messaging rates may apply.

Send & Receive   4 Addresses >

SMS/MMS

MMS Messaging

HOT TIP: If you want to allow others to be notified when you have read their messages, enable Send Read Receipts.

ALERT: If you have a pay-per-text messaging plan from your service provider, be careful how many texts you send to other cell phone users who do not use an iPhone. The cost of the texts will soon add up.

Write or dictate a text message

You can send a text message to virtually anyone. You can send a text by typing a phone number, email address, or a contact name your iPhone recognises. To make sure you don't get charged by your cell phone data provider, send your text to a contact who also uses Messages on a compatible iDevice; this is an iMessage.

1 Tap Messages.

2 Tap the Compose button.

3 Type a cell phone number, a contact name or an email address.

4 Tap inside the iMessage or Text Message window and then type or dictate your message.

5 Tap Send.

1 Messages

Messages 2

New Message   Cancel

To: Mary Cosmo 3

I'm out front! 4   5 Send

HOT TIP: If you don't have an iPhone, iPad or iPod touch contact but want to test the Messages app, send a text to me (joliballew@gmail.com).

! ALERT: Although you can send a text to any phone number, it won't arrive there unless the phone is capable of receiving texts. You can't send a text to a home phone on a landline, for instance.

WHAT DOES THIS MEAN?
If the text window shows **iMessage**, you are texting another iDevice user. This is free over Wi-Fi. If the text window shows **Text Message** instead, you are texting someone who does not use an iDevice and you will be charged (or the text will be counted towards your data plan's text limit).

Send a photo in a message

There is a camera icon located on the left of the Text Message window. You can tap this to take or choose a picture to send with your message. The message becomes a multimedia message when you do this (as opposed to a text message).

1 Compose a text as outlined in the previous section. You can add multiple recipients.

2 Tap the camera icon.

3 Choose Take Photo or Video, or Choose Existing.

4 Do what is required to take or select the photo.

5 Tap Send.

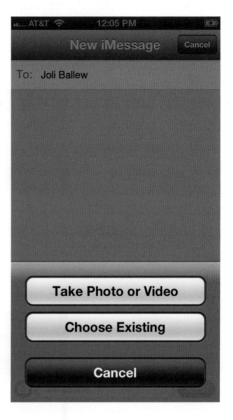

! ALERT: Some data providers charge more to send and receive multimedia messages than they do to send and receive simple text messages. If you (or a contact) are on a pay-as-you-go texting plan and you aren't sending the message as an iMessage, keep this in mind.

? DID YOU KNOW?
Some cell phone users can receive text messages but cannot receive multimedia messages. This is because they do not have a data plan associated with their cell phone. Unfortunately, you won't receive an error that the message did not go through.

Let Siri write your message

It's much more fun to let Siri send your text message than it is to type it. Siri can only send messages that contain text, but often this is all you need. Siri recognises all manner of requests. Close the Messages app (just to get the full effect), hold down the Home button to engage Siri, and try the following:

1 'I need to send a message to someone' – Siri will tell you to give him a contact's name, a phone number or an email address, then he'll ask what you want to say.

> To whom shall I send it? (I need a contact name, phone number or email address.)

2 'Send a message to <say recipient's name>' – Siri will ask what the message should say, and you can tell him.

3 'I need to tell "recipient" I'm running late'.

> Here's your message to Mary Cosmo.
>
> To: Mary Cosmo
>
> I'll be late
>
> Cancel   Send

! ALERT: After Siri writes your message, you'll have to answer Siri to let him know you want to send it, or you'll need to tap Send.

🔥 HOT TIP: If Siri doesn't get your message right, tap Cancel and try again.

Add a contact

You've read about contacts in lots of places in this text. You email a contact. You call a contact. You can assign a picture to a contact card. And as you learned earlier, you can tell Siri to send a message to a contact. That contact must already have been entered or synced if Siri is to find it.

Contacts

1 Tap the Phone icon.

2 Tap the Contacts tab.

3 Tap the + sign (not shown).

4 Type as much information about the contact as you can. (Tap the red dash to delete an entry.)

5 Tap Add Photo and choose a photo to use (or take one).

6 Scroll down to the bottom and tap Add Field. Add and edit the desired field.

7 Tap Done.

AT&T 12:10 PM

Cancel **New Contact** Done

⊖ anniversary	**October 8, 2012**
other	Date
⊖ Twitter	**@joliballew**
Flickr	User Name
⊖ messages	**joli_ballew@hotmail.com**
	Skype
work	User Name
	Skype
⊕	add field

? DID YOU KNOW?
During the creation of or while editing a contact card, you can tap any category title (home or mobile, for instance) to change it to something else (main, pager or iPhone, for instance).

🔥 HOT TIP: You can access your Contacts list from the Phone app or the Contacts app. The Contacts app may be located on a secondary Home screen, so accessing them from the Phone icon is often easier.

? DID YOU KNOW?
Siri can't create contacts for you.

Use a contact card to communicate with a contact

You can initiate communications with a contact using the contact's card, available from the Contacts tab of the Phone app. The options available to you depend on how much information you've input.

1 Tap a Facebook entry to open Safari and visit the contact's Facebook profile.

2 Tap a Twitter name to send a tweet or view their tweets.

```
.ıı... AT&T 📶        11:50 AM            🔋

‹ All Contacts    Unified Info        Edit

  ┌─────────────────────────────────────┐
  │ Facebook  joliballew                 │
  ├─────────────────────────────────────┤
  │ Twitter  @JoliBallew                 │
  ├─────────────────────────────────────┤
  │ Facebook  Joli Ballew               │
  └─────────────────────────────────────┘

  ┌─────────────────────────────────────┐
  │ home  joliballew@gmail.com           │
  ├─────────────────────────────────────┤
  │ IM  joli.ballew (Facebook)           │
  └─────────────────────────────────────┘

  ┌──────────────────┐  ┌──────────────────┐
  │  Send Message    │  │    FaceTime      │
  └──────────────────┘  └──────────────────┘

  ┌──────────────────┐  ┌──────────────────┐
  │  Share Contact   │  │  Add to Favorites│
  └──────────────────┘  └──────────────────┘

  Linked Contacts

★          🕐         👤          ⁝⁝⁝        ⌒○
Favorites  Recents   Contacts   Keypad   Voicemail
```

HOT TIP: Try tapping other entries besides those mentioned here. You can tap a phone number to place a call, for instance, or tap a web address to visit their website.

3 Tap Send Message to text the contact; FaceTime to start a FaceTime conversation.

4 Tap Share Contact to send the contact's information to someone else.

5 Tap Add to Favorites to make the contact card appear in the Favorites list.

6 Tap the Address to open Maps and get directions to the contact's address.

HOT TIP: Add new information for a contact as it arrives, so you'll always have access to multiple ways to contact them.

Link contacts

At some point you'll likely encounter an all-to-familiar problem. You'll have multiple contact cards for a single contact. Perhaps one card holds an email address, another a phone number and another a mailing address. You can link these cards so that all of the information is available in a single place (although it's probably better to delete all but one contact card and input the desired information manually into a single card). Once linked (or properly managed) you should see only one entry for the contact in the Contacts list.

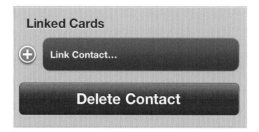

1 Tap a duplicate contact card.

2 Tap Edit.

3 Scroll down to the end of the card and tap Link Contact.

4 Tap the desired card to link; tap Link. Repeat as desired.

5 Tap Done.

HOT TIP: You may want to link different people, perhaps a husband and wife.

HOT TIP: Delete duplicate contact cards you don't need or that don't offer any additional information.

Use Passbook

The Passbook app lets you access coupons, store cards, boarding passes, tickets, and more. To make this work you must get an app from the App Store that is 'Passbook' compatible. After that, you must make a purchase, download coupons, or perform some other compatible task to view the data in the Passbook app.

1 Tap Passbook to open the Passbook app.

2 Tap App Store.

3 Locate and download compatible Passbook apps.

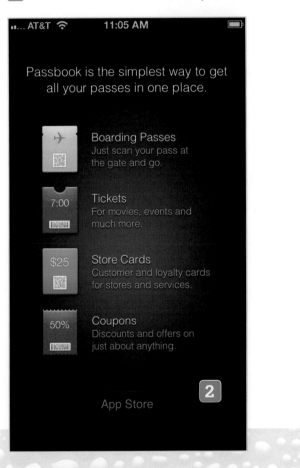

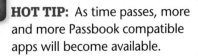

ALERT: Apps that are Passbook compatible will require you to create an account and log in with it.

HOT TIP: As time passes, more and more Passbook compatible apps will become available.

Dictate a note

The Notes app lets you type or dictate notes to yourself or others. Once a note is written, you can view it, share it via email, print it to a compatible printer or delete it. Notes is an iCloud-compatible app.

1 Tap Notes on the Home screen.

2 If you've enabled Notes for compatible email accounts and/or iCloud, you'll have options for where you'd like to save the note. If applicable, tap an entry here.

Accounts	+
All Notes	>
Gmail	>
Yahoo!	>
iCloud	>

3 Tap the + sign to start a new note.

? DID YOU KNOW?

Some email accounts, such as ones from Google and Yahoo!, enable you to take notes, save and sync them, just as you can with iCloud on your iPhone.

4 Type or dictate your note.

5 Tap Done (to hide the keyboard and leave the note active) or Notes (to see a list of Notes).

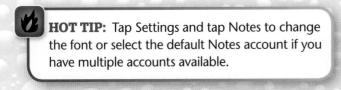

HOT TIP: Tap Settings and tap Notes to change the font or select the default Notes account if you have multiple accounts available.

Let Siri compose your note

If you're of a certain age, or if you watch old movies, you may have heard a boss tell his secretary to 'take a note'. Although this may not be appropriate terminology in the workplace any more, Siri doesn't mind being told to take a note one bit!

1 Tap and hold the Home button to engage Siri.

2 Say, 'Siri, take a note'. (You could also say, 'Make a note to <...>' and Siri will oblige.

> OK, I can take that note for you... just tell me what you want it to say.

3 Tell Siri what you'd like the note to say.

4 Siri will create the note. Tap it, if desired, to open Notes and add more information or edit the note.

> Here's your note:
>
> Consider remodeling the kitchen

HOT TIP: Although you can use Notes for to-do lists, Reminders might be better (detailed next).

? DID YOU KNOW?
You can use the Notes app to paste data you've copied from other sources. For instance, you can copy a recipe from a cookery website and paste it into a note to make it available later.

Let Siri compose a reminder

You can tell Siri to remind you to do something specific at a certain time. When it's time to do whatever you've asked to be reminded about, an alert will appear on your iPhone and a sound will play. Reminders you've configured also appear in the Notifications area, as you'll learn in the next section.

1 Tell Siri to remind you to do something. You can say something like:

- 'I'm sleepy. Wake me up in one hour.'
- 'Remind me to mow the lawn early on Sunday morning.'
- 'Remind me to pick up my dry cleaning after work today.'

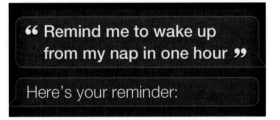

2 Confirm the reminder.

? **DID YOU KNOW?**

You can configure reminders manually from inside the Reminders app.

3 For fun, open the Reminders app on the Home screen to view the reminder. This is not necessary.

HOT TIP: The Reminders app is a good place to create to-do lists, because you can check them off when you've completed the tasks set down.

View reminders in the Notifications bar

Although Siri will remind you with a pop-up when a reminder has come due, as shown here, you can check your upcoming reminders from the Notifications area. You can access this from any screen.

1 Place your finger at the top of the screen.

2 Drag downwards.

3 Note the list of reminders (and other notifications).

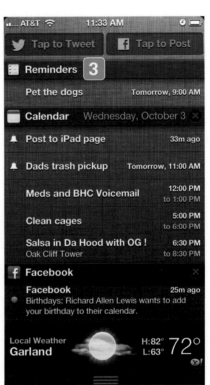

? DID YOU KNOW?
You can tap any reminder in the Notifications area to open the Reminders app with that reminder in red text.

HOT TIP: Siri can't delete reminders once they're created. To delete a reminder, open the Reminders app, tap the reminder, and then tap Delete.

View and manage reminders from the Reminders app

You can use the Reminders app to view all of your reminders, mark reminders as completed, delete reminders, view reminders in various ways, configure reminders to repeat, and even write notes about the reminder. You can even create new Reminders lists. There isn't enough space here to cover all of this, but try the following inside the Reminders app.

1 Tap in the box beside a reminder to mark it complete.

2 Tap a reminder to view its Details page, where you can add information to the reminder.

3 Tap Remind Me At a Location to be reminded to do something when you leave or arrive at that location. Click Done or Cancel.

Reminders

☐ Water needs to be changed to Tuesdays and
10/6/12, 9:00 AM, Weekly

.... AT&T 📶 11:36 AM 🕐 ▭

Cancel **Details** Done

Water needs to be changed to Tuesdays and

Remind Me On a Day **ON**

Saturday, Oct 6, 2012, 9:00 AM

Repeat Weekly >

End Repeat Never >

Remind Me At a Location OFF

Show More...

Delete

4 Tap the icon with the horizontal lines to access additional options. Note you can create new lists here.

5 Continue exploring, and then tap Done.

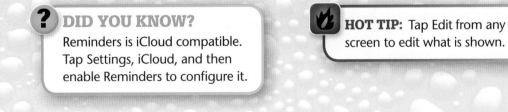

HOT TIP: Tap Edit from any screen to edit what is shown.

Configure iCloud for the apps you use

For good measure, take one more look at the iCloud options in Settings and enable the iCloud-compatible apps you plan to use in the long term.

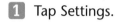 Tap Settings.

 Tap iCloud.

 Configure settings as desired.

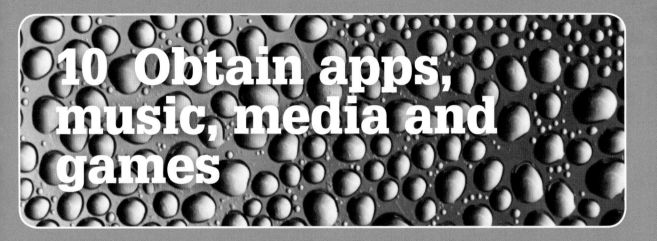

10 Obtain apps, music, media and games

Introduction

You have access to a lot of built-in apps such as Maps, Messages, Music and Calendar, among others. As you know, apps help you to do things, such as send email, get directions or schedule events and appointments. You can buy or obtain more apps from the App Store. Whatever you want to do with your iPhone, there's probably an app for that!

You also have access to a lot of media on your iPhone. These include wallpapers, ringtones and your own personal music, photos and videos. You can get more media from the iTunes Store. You may want to purchase songs or albums, movies, TV shows, ringtones and so on.

In this chapter you'll learn how to get new apps, media and even games. You acquire these items in a manner similar to acquiring books from the iBookstore or courses from iTunes U: you navigate to the item you want and work through the purchasing process. It's important to note that free media is available if you're not ready to spend any money yet.

Explore the App Store

You get apps from the App Store. The App Store is available from the Home screen. The App Store, like other apps you've used previously, has tabs and categories to explore, and as you navigate, various 'back' buttons appear.

App Store

1 Tap the App Store icon on the Home screen.

2 Tap each tab and explore what's available for each:

- Featured – To view editor's favourites, new apps, the hottest apps and more.
- Charts – To sort the most popular apps by how many times they've been downloaded and/or purchased.
- Genius – To get recommendations from Apple based on your previous purchases.
- Search – To search for an app by name.
- Updates – To obtain updates to apps you've already installed.

3 Tap Charts to access the most popular apps. Leave this open for the next tasks.

HOT TIP: You get apps from the App Store. You do not get music, movies, TV shows, books and the like here.

HOT TIP: If there's a 'back' button showing on any screen (Categories isn't one), tap it. You want to view the landing pages for each tab introduced here (not an app's Details page, for instance).

Get a free app

One of the tabs in the App Store is Charts. This is a great place to get your first app because you know the apps listed here are popular, and one of the available options is Top Free.

 Tap App Store on the Home screen.

 Tap the Charts tab at the bottom of the screen.

 Use your finger to flick left and right through the free apps shown.

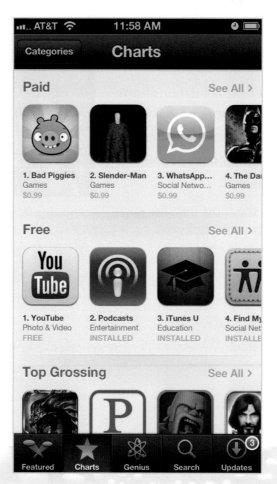

WHAT DOES THIS MEAN?

App: A small program that enables you to do something. You can keep track of the calories you eat in a day, play a game, post a picture to Facebook, subscribe to a music service and even download a web browser to replace Safari.

4 Tap any app you find interesting. (We'll choose YouTube.)

5 If you decide you want an app, tap Free, then Install App, type your password and tap OK.

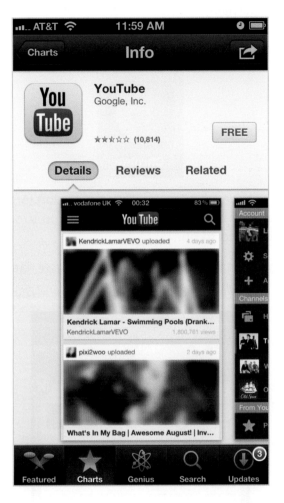

ALERT: What you see in the list of top apps changes often; what you see won't match what's shown here.

Use the free app

Once an app has finished installing, you tap it to open it. You'll find it on the last available secondary Home screen.

1 Tap the new app's icon on the appropriate Home screen.

2 Accept any terms of service, allow or disallow permission for the app to post to social networks, enable or disable the ability for the app to send you badges, alerts and 'push' notifications and so on.

3 If prompted, type your email and password, enter a user name and allow the app to gain access to your location, as desired.

4 If prompted, take a tour, read the directions, choose an icon to represent your player, etc. Here we're watching a YouTube video.

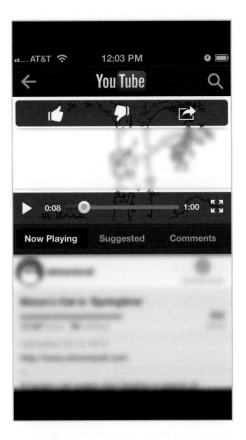

! ALERT: If an app wants your permission to post 'on your behalf' to Facebook to Twitter, think twice before you grant it the ability to do so. You won't know how much (or what) the app will post until after the fact.

? DID YOU KNOW? Often an app will offer configuration options in Settings (but not always).

WHAT DOES THIS MEAN?
Badges, alerts, push notifications: These, and other such options, should be enabled if you want or need the app to let you know when it's your turn to play, when you've met a specific threshold or when there's a breaking news alert, among other things.

Search for an app

Often you'll know the name of the app you want to install. If so, you can search for the app.

1 Open the App Store and tap the Search tab.

2 Type the name of the app.

3 Carefully review the results and choose the appropriate one.

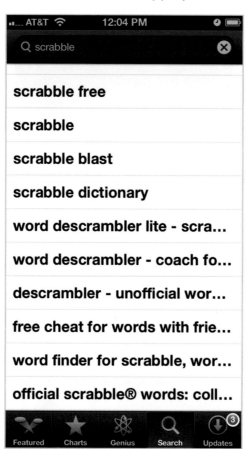

Get app updates

The App Store icon on the Home screen may have a number on it, as shown here. If so, there are updates available for one or more of the apps you already own. Updates may fix problems with the app or offer new features, or both.

 Tap the App Store icon.

 Tap the Updates tab.

 Tap Update All. (You could update specific apps one at a time, if you'd rather.)

4 Input your password and tap OK.

5 Wait while the updates install.

HOT TIP: Note the Purchased option under the Updates tab. To see what you've purchased and to re-download any app you've uninstalled, tap here.

HOT TIP: If you see a number on the Newsstand, open the App Store and tap the Updates tab. Look for updates there.

Uninstall and reinstall apps

You won't like every app you acquire, and you may download a free app and then later download the paid version of it. You may also 'complete' an app, perhaps by getting to the highest level of a game. Whatever the reason, at some point you'll probably want to uninstall an app.

1 Tap and hold the icon for the app you want to remove from your iPhone.

2 When the X appears, tap it.

3 Tap Delete; tap the Home button.

4 To reinstall the app later, either:

- Find it in the App Store and tap Install, or
- From the App Store, tap Updates, then Purchased, and then tap the app to reinstall.

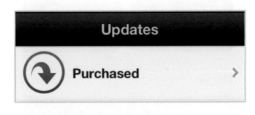

HOT TIP: If you have problems with an app, such as it freezing during use or not opening, delete and reinstall it.

? DID YOU KNOW?
You can uninstall a paid app and reinstall it without paying for it again.

Explore iTunes

You buy and rent media from the iTunes Store, although you'll find free media as well. iTunes is available from the Home screen. iTunes, like other apps, offers tabs, categories and various 'back' buttons to assist in navigation.

1 From the Home screen, tap iTunes.

2 Tap the following tabs and note what's on each screen:

- Music – To access new releases, top-selling songs and albums, sort music by genre, and more.

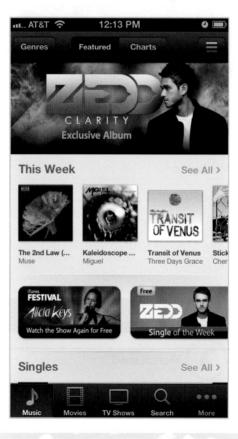

! ALERT: iTunes, on your computer, is a program that lets you manage your media, play it and also shop in the store. iTunes on your iPhone just offers access to the iTunes Store.

- Movies – To access movies and videos.
- TV Shows – To access TV shows, including season premiers and hits, among other things.
- Search – To search for something specific.
- More – To access other types of media, including but not limited to (ring, text and alert) tones, Genius suggestions, audiobooks, purchased items and more.

More	Edit
🎧 **Audiobooks**	›
🔔 **Tones**	›
⚛ **Genius**	›

Search for a song or album

You can look for just about any media imaginable from the Search tab of iTunes. You can search for a movie or song title, or for work by a particular artist or actor, for instance.

1 From inside iTunes, tap the Search tab.

2 Type the desired keywords. Tap any result or tap Search. View the results.

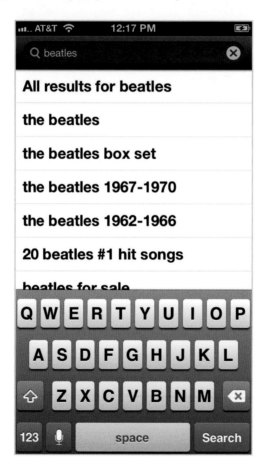

3 Tap any entry to view the Details page.

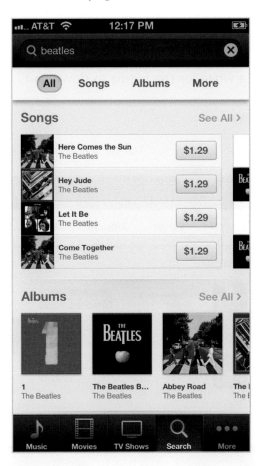

4 Tap the appropriate option to make a purchase, hear a preview or to return to the previous page.

ALERT: Audiobooks are probably the most expensive media you'll encounter, followed closely by entire seasons of TV shows and full length feature movies.

Buy media

You buy media the same way as you buy apps and books. You locate what you want and tap the price button. The big difference with buying media (as opposed to, say, books), is that it can take a while for the media to download.

1 Locate the media to buy.

2 Tap the price button.

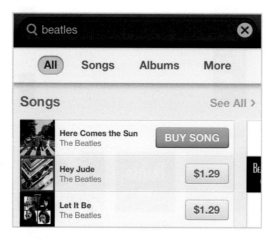

3 Tap the Buy button, type your password and tap OK.

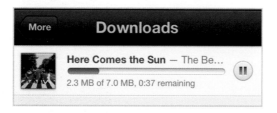

4 Tap More and then tap Downloads to view the download process(es), if applicable.

Rent a movie

If you want to watch a movie but have no reason to purchase it, oftentimes you can rent it. To find out if you can, navigate to the movie you want to watch and tap to view its Details page. If Rent is an option, tap it and complete the checkout and download process.

- When you rent a movie you have 30 days to start watching it.

- Once you start to watch it you have 24 hours to complete it in the US or 48 hours in Europe.

- You can watch the movie as many times as you want while inside your 24- or 48-hour window.

- The rental is deleted from your phone once the rental period ends.

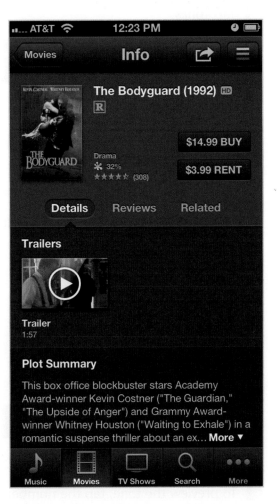

 HOT TIP: If you're really into watching movies on your iPhone, consider Netflix. For less than it costs to buy a single movie from iTunes, you can have access to thousands of movies on Netflix, with unlimited time to view them. The Netflix app is available from the App Store.

Get a new ringtone

You get 'tones' from the iTunes Store, from the More tab's landing page. You may have to tap the 'back' button to get here if you've navigated away from it.

1 From iTunes, tap More.

2 Tap Tones.

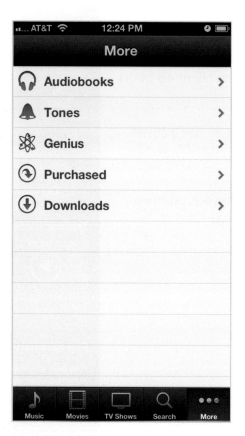

3 Navigate to a tone that interests you.

4 To preview the tone, tap the number listed to the left of its title on the Details page.

HOT TIP: If you apply the tone to a contact, you can access the tone and change it from the Contacts list.

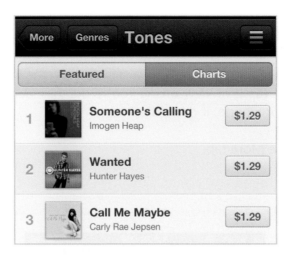

5 If you decide to buy the tone, tap the price button and decide how to use the tone.

New Tone

"Someone's Calling"

Set as Default Ringtone

Assign to a Contact

Done

6 Type your password and tap OK.

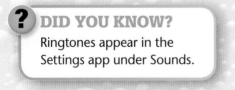

? DID YOU KNOW?

Ringtones appear in the Settings app under Sounds.

View purchased media

You may have noticed the Purchased option available from the More tab inside the iTunes app. You can tap it to view media you've purchased. You can download purchased media to your iPhone, if desired.

1 From iTunes, tap the More tab.

2 Tap Purchased.

3 Tap the desired entry.

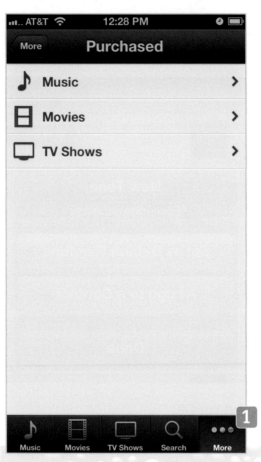

ALERT: Movies require a lot of storage space and can quickly fill up your phone. Only download movies you'll watch soon, and delete them when you're finished.

4 Navigate to the item to download.

5 Tap the cloud icon to download the media.

Open Game Center

Game Center is another app that comes pre-installed on your iPhone. To use it, you sign in with your Apple ID, obtain and/or play some games, and keep track of your scores and achievements.

1. Tap Game Center to open it. When prompted with setup questions, answer as desired.

2. Sign in.

3 Explore each tab. If you've downloaded Game Center compatible games, you'll see them from the Games tab.

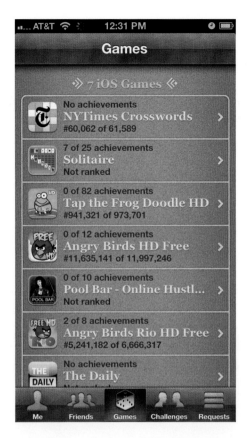

Download a game

Although you can go directly to the App Store to locate games for your iPhone, it may be better to use Game Center. You can browse recommendations, make sure you're getting Game Center compatible games, get recommendations from your Game Center friends, and more.

1 Tap Game Center to open it. Sign in if prompted.

2 Tap Games, Scroll down if necessary, and tap Find Game Center Games.

3 From the results, locate a game to acquire.

4 Work through the purchasing and download process.

5 You can now access the game from Game Center.

6 You may be prompted to be matched with another player or invite a friend.

? DID YOU KNOW?
Some Game Center games are multiplayer games. You can play against friends or ask to be matched up with strangers.

! ALERT: Be careful when playing games. You may be prompted to buy things like aeroplanes, bombs, farm animals and so on, and the costs can add up.

11 Secure and back up your iPhone

Introduction

There are many ways to secure and back up your iPhone, and you've explored some of them already. You know how to save and sync contacts to iCloud, for instance, and you know how to sync your iPhone with your computer to create regular backups. You may already know that you can require a passcode to unlock your phone when you want to use it, too.

However, because the security tips you've learned so far have been scattered throughout this text, and because we want to make sure your iPhone is really secure before we leave you on your own, we'll close by repeating a few of the security options you may already have explored, and several you've likely never heard of.

Before you start, take a moment to consider some things you can do to physically protect your phone. You can purchase a hard shell case, keep the phone in your purse or pocket when you aren't using it, be careful not to leave your phone on the bar at a pub, avoid letting your phone get too cold or hot, and hang on to your phone tightly while near water.

Understand Location Services

Some apps need to know your approximate location to function efficiently and effectively. For instance, Maps can't tell you where the closest coffee shop is (without specific input from you) if it can't figure out where you are. Weather apps, local news apps, websites, and more, also use your location to personalise your experience. Some people feel this is an invasion of privacy, while others see it as a valid necessity and convenience.

1 The first time you use an app you may be prompted to let it learn your location.

2 If you don't allow this, and you decide later you'd like to, you'll have to do so from the Settings app, from Privacy and Location Services.

! ALERT: Some apps that you use to send messages, social updates and the like may post your location automatically. This can be a security issue. If you find this happens, disable Location Services for that app in Settings and uninstall the app if that doesn't work.

3 Some apps ask for permission to use your location when in reality there's no need. As an example, a dictionary or thesaurus app really has no need to know where you are.

4 You can disable Location Services for specific apps from Settings > Privacy > Location Services.

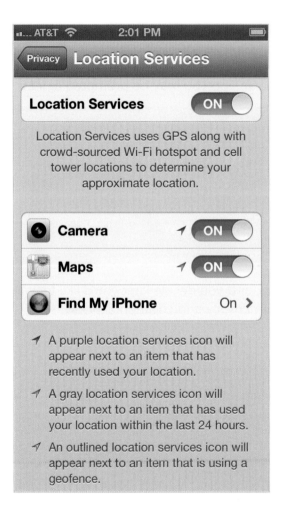

ALERT: It's probably a good idea to completely disable Location Services on a child's iPhone. Instruct the child how to enable this for Maps though, should they ever get lost and need to find their way home.

Configure Auto-Lock

Your iPhone becomes inactive and the screen goes dark after one minute. You can change this to something longer, although it isn't advisable. Longer wake times will use up your battery more quickly than shorter ones, and when the phone is active and available, anyone can use it.

1 From the Home screen, tap Settings.

2 Tap General and then Auto-Lock.

Auto-Lock	3 Minutes ›
Passcode Lock	On ›
Restrictions	Off ›

3 Configure the desired amount of time.

General Auto-Lock	
1 Minute	✓
2 Minutes	
3 Minutes	
4 Minutes	
5 Minutes	
Never	

 ALERT: Unless you configure a passcode lock (detailed next), your phone will always be unsecured.

HOT TIP: You may want to leave your phone active longer if you're playing a game and waiting for another player to make a move.

Configure a passcode lock

Your iPhone will lock automatically after the time configured in the Auto-Lock settings, and you can lock the phone manually by pressing the On/Off button one time. A passcode lock is a four-digit number you configure that must be input to unlock the phone once it's been locked.

1 Tap Settings, General, then Passcode Lock.

2 Tap Turn Passcode On.

3 Type the desired code twice.

4 Tap Require Passcode.

5 Tap how long to wait after the phone is idle before requiring the code. Immediately is the safest.

Settings	**General**
Auto-Lock	1 Minute **>**
Passcode Lock **1**	Off **>**
Restrictions	Off **>**

General	**Passcode Lock**

Turn Passcode On **2**

Change Passcode

Require Passcode After 15 min. **>**

Simple Passcode ON

A simple passcode is a 4 digit number.

Passcode Lock	**Require Passcode**

Immediately ✓

After 1 minute **5**

After 5 minutes

HOT TIP: Don't share the password associated with your Apple ID with anyone, and only share your passcode lock with your spouse or a close relative.

? DID YOU KNOW?
You can disable the Simple Passcode requirement in favour of a more complex code. When you do, you can choose a password that consists of letters, numbers and special characters, which is more secure.

Opt to erase data after 10 failed logon attempts

There is an option you can enable in the Passcode Lock settings to have all data erased from your iPhone after 10 failed attempts to unlock it. You may think this is a drastic measure, but it isn't. If you use iCloud or iTunes to back up the data on your phone, you can restore it easily. We suggest you enable this feature.

1 Tap Settings, General, then Passcode Lock.

2 Enter your passcode lock.

3 Scroll down and move the slider for Erase Data from Off to On.

4 Tap Enable to verify.

.ıl... AT&T 📶	2:05 PM	🔋

General Passcode Lock

Require Passcode	After 15 min. ❯
Simple Passcode	ON

A simple passcode is a 4 digit number.

Allow Access When Locked:

Siri	ON
Passbook	ON
Reply with Message	ON

Erase Data **3**	ON

Erase all data on this iPhone
after 10 failed passcode attempts.

Data protection is enabled.

! ALERT: You probably shouldn't enable this feature if you don't back up your iPhone to your computer or to iCloud.

▶ SEE ALSO: See the sections Back up with iTunes, and Enable iCloud backups, later in this chapter.

Configure Restrictions

Restrictions enable you to hide specific apps from the Home screen, thus making them inaccessible. You may want to enable restrictions on a child's phone to keep them from accessing certain applications, among other things.

1 Tap Settings, General, then Restrictions.

2 Tap Enable Restrictions.

3 Enter a passcode (twice) for setting Restrictions. Use something other than your iPhone's Lock screen passcode.

4 Turn on or off apps as desired.

Passcode Lock	On >
Restrictions	Off >

⌐.... AT&T 🤖 2:08 PM ▭

General Restrictions

Disable Restrictions

Allow:

Safari	OFF
Camera	ON
FaceTime	OFF
iTunes	OFF
iBookstore	ON
Installing Apps	ON
Deleting Apps	OFF
Siri	ON
Explicit Language	ON

?  **DID YOU KNOW?**
Scroll down to the bottom of the Restrictions page to see additional options.

? **DID YOU KNOW?**
Beyond hiding apps from the Home screen you can also set restrictions based on media ratings, and you can disable in-app purchases.

🔥 HOT TIP: If you don't want your youngster playing multiplayer games in Game Center, disable this feature.

Back up with iTunes

You already know how to sync your iPhone with iTunes (see Chapter 1). When you do, a backup is created. You should back up your iPhone using iTunes at least once a month.

1 Connect your iPhone to your computer using the USB cable that came with it.

2 From the Summary tab, select Back up to this computer, if it is not already selected. (When the backup completes, return the setting to its original configuration, if applicable.)

3 Wait while the backup completes.

4 If it does not appear that a backup has taken place, right-click your iPhone in the left pane and click Back Up.

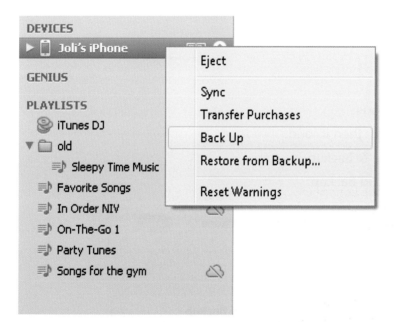

ALERT: The backup option shown here may be greyed out. If so, wait for the current processes to end and try again.

HOT TIP: Even if you enable the option to back up to iCloud, perform this task once a month anyway, just for good measure.

Enable iCloud backups

You already know that you can enable specific data to be synced with iCloud for safekeeping (Mail, Contacts, Calendars, Reminders and so on). You may not have enabled iCloud Backup though. You should enable this feature if you do not have a computer for backing up your iPhone, or if you'd like a secondary protective measure in place.

1 If you use a computer to sync:

- Connect your iPhone to your computer and select it in the left pane of iTunes.
- From the Summary tab, tick Back up to iCloud.
- Complete any other requirements.

Backup

- ⦿ Back up to iCloud
- ○ Back up to this computer
- ☐ Encrypt local backup Change Password...

Last backed up to iCloud: Yesterday 8:55 PM

2 From your iPhone:

- Tap Settings, then iCloud.
- Tap Storage & Backup.
- Enable iCloud Backup.

Find My iPhone   ON

Find My iPhone allows you to locate this iPhone on a map and remotely lock or erase it.

Storage & Backup   ❯

? DID YOU KNOW?

Some people believe that saving data to iCloud is a bad idea. They wonder if Apple is somehow viewing their data and if the data itself is safe and secure. We think iCloud is fine to use and have no issues with it.

? DID YOU KNOW?

If you go over your limit of 5 GB in iCloud and want to buy more, you can.

Enable Find My iPhone

If you have not yet enabled Find My iPhone, you should. Once enabled, if your iPhone is ever lost or stolen, and it is turned on, you can find out where it is from any computer or compatible Internet-connected device. You can also send a message, erase the data, and more, all from a remote location.

 1 Tap Settings, then iCloud.

2 Next to Find My iPhone, move the slider from Off to On.

3 Tap Allow.

🔥 **HOT TIP:** Work through the next section now so you'll know how to locate your iPhone should you ever lose it.

⚠ **ALERT:** If a thief steals your phone and turns it off, you won't be able to find your iPhone using Find My iPhone.

Test Find My iPhone

With Find My iPhone enabled, test it. Leave the phone on, and place it somewhere out of sight. You may want to place it in another room of your house or perhaps somewhere in your car.

1 From any computer, navigate to www.icloud.com. Log in with your Apple ID and password.

2 Click Find My iPhone.

3 Click Devices. Click your lost device.

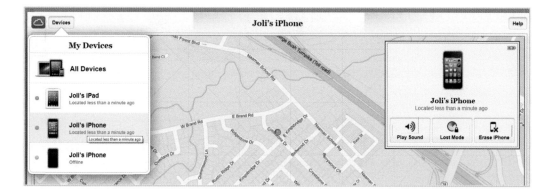

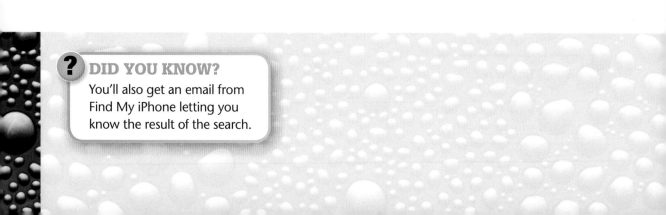

? DID YOU KNOW?

You'll also get an email from Find My iPhone letting you know the result of the search.

4 Note the options. For this exercise, click Play Sound.

5 On your iPhone, note the message.

6 Now, from www.icloud.com, click Lost Mode. Note the options.

! **ALERT:** If you know someone has stolen your phone, don't send a message or sound; instead, erase the data on your iPhone as soon as possible.

Restore a replacement phone

If you've created the proper backups, you can restore a replacement phone with the data easily. It's part of the set-up process.

1 When you first turn on your new iPhone, log in with your existing Apple ID and password.

2 Know where your backups are; they are in iCloud or on your computer in iTunes.

3 When prompted, choose to populate the phone with data from a backup.

4 Choose the desired backup location. You will have to connect your iPhone to your computer to use one from iTunes.

5 If you can't restore from a backup for any reason and you have a backup in iTunes, connect your phone, right-click your iPhone in the left pane, and click Restore from Backup.

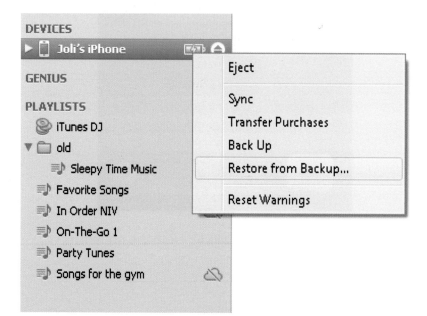

? DID YOU KNOW?
It takes quite a while to restore your iPhone from a backup using iTunes. Be patient.

🔥 HOT TIP: Never be afraid to erase all of the data on your iPhone if you have good backups. The restore process may take some time, but it's simple to do.

Reset your phone

You can reset parts of your iPhone to factory defaults, such as the order of the apps on the Home screen, your network settings and more. You can also reset the entire phone to factory defaults. You should do this when you're ready to sell the phone or pass it on to someone else.

1 Tap Settings, General, then Reset.

2 Choose what you want to reset. If you're getting rid of the phone, choose Erase All Content and Settings.

3 If required, input your passcode lock and verify your decision.

ALERT: Do not choose Erase All Content and Settings unless you are ready to sell your phone or give it away.

HOT TIP: If you want the main Home screen to look like it did when you first got it, choose to reset the Home screen layout.

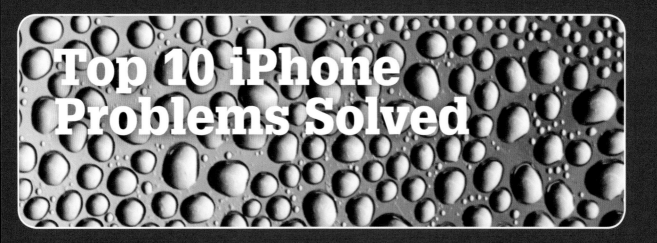

Top 10 iPhone Problems Solved

Problem 1: I can't sync over Wi-Fi

You can sync your iPhone with your computer automatically over Wi-Fi without physically connecting it, provided certain criteria are met. You enable this from iTunes on your computer, from the Summary tab, while your iPhone is connected.

1 In iTunes, from the Summary tab, enable Sync with this iPhone over Wi-Fi. Click Apply. (Apply won't be available if criteria can't be met by your computer or network.)

iTunes Match	**Backup**
Ping	
Purchased	○ Back up to iCloud
Purchased on Joli's iPad	○ Back up to this computer
DEVICES	☐ Encrypt local backup [Change Password...]
▶ 🗋 Joli's iPhone ⏏	Last backed up to iCloud: Today 8:41 AM
GENIUS	
PLAYLISTS	**Options**
iTunes DJ	
▼ 🗀 old	☑ Open iTunes when this iPhone is connected
Sleepy Time Music	☑ Sync with this iPhone over Wi-Fi
Favorite Songs	☐ Sync only checked songs and videos
In Order NIV	☐ Prefer standard definition videos
On-The-Go 1	☐ Convert higher bit rate songs to [128 kbps ▾] AAC
Party Tunes	☐ Manually manage music and videos
Songs for the gym	

2 Detach your iPhone from the computer.

3 Plug your iPhone into an electrical outlet.

4 Verify the computer is turned on and iTunes is running.

5 Tap Settings > General > iTunes Wi-Fi Sync, and tap Sync now.

? DID YOU KNOW?
When these criteria are met, your iPhone will sync automatically and without prompting or intervention once a day.

! ALERT: The computer and the iPhone must be connected to the same Wi-Fi network you used to configure Wi-Fi syncing.

Problem 2: How can I put a person on hold, 'Press 1 to continue' and perform similar in-call tasks?

When you are on a call you will occasionally need to do something else at the same time. Perhaps you need to put someone on hold, 'Press 1 to continue', add someone to the call or look up contact information. You can do all of this and more. The screen that holds these options appears automatically when you remove the phone from your ear.

1 Mute – in essence, to put the call on hold by muting your outgoing speaker. When mute is enabled, you can continue to talk (perhaps to a colleague in the same room) but the person on the other end of the line can't hear what you are saying.

2 Keypad – To access the keypad in order to press a number as prompted by an operator. Tap Hide Keypad to return to the controls.

3 Speaker – To place the call on speaker, so you can free your hands for other tasks or to let others around you hear the conversation.

4 Add call – To add another caller to the conversation.

5 FaceTime – To switch to a FaceTime conversation.

6 Contacts – To access your Contacts list, perhaps to look up contact information.

 SEE ALSO: For more information about FaceTime, refer to Chapter 8.

HOT TIP: If you get a lot of phone calls, consider a hands-free Bluetooth headset.

Problem 3: I can't connect my Bluetooth headset

A Bluetooth device is one that you can connect to your iPhone and that can communicate with it wirelessly. You may have a hands-free headset that fits this category. These headsets (or earpieces) enable you to answer phone calls without touching your iPhone or even looking at it.

1 Turn on the Bluetooth device you want to connect.

2 On your iPhone, tap Settings and then Bluetooth.

3 Move the slider from off to on.

4 When the iPhone finds the device, tap it.

5 Follow the rest of the instructions to pair the device. Here, a keyboard is paired.

! ALERT: Turn off Bluetooth when you don't need it. Bluetooth can drain your battery.

? DID YOU KNOW?
There are lots of kinds of Bluetooth devices, including keyboards. If you are in the market for one, make sure it's iPhone 5 compatible before you buy it.

🔥 HOT TIP: When you finish configuring settings in the Settings app, tap the 'back' button the necessary number of times to return to the main Settings screen. This will make the settings quickly available next time you need them.

Problem 4: I've been to places on the Internet I don't want anyone else to know about

You can delete the items in the History list and any data that Safari has saved from Settings.

1 From the Home screen, tap Settings.

2 Tap Safari.

3 Tap Clear History, and Clear History again to verify.

4 Repeat to clear Cookies and Data.

.ıı. AT&T 📶   11:56 AM

Settings   **Safari**

Open Links   In New Page **>**

Privacy

Private Browsing   OFF

Accept Cookies   From visited **>**

Clear History

Clear Cookies and Data

Are you sure you want to clear history? This cannot be undone.

Use Cellular Da

Clear History

Cancel

Fraud Warning

🔥 **HOT TIP:** To access History in Safari, tap the Bookmarks icon and tap History (you may have to tap an applicable 'back' button to get there).

❓ **DID YOU KNOW?**
You can also clear your History list from the list itself. Tap Bookmarks, History, then Clear.

Problem 5: I took a great photo but it needs to be edited a little. What can I do?

Yes, you can lightly edit photos using your iPhone! Editing options include rotating the image, applying auto enhancements, fixing red-eye and cropping the image.

1 Locate any photo to edit and tap it. It should be in full screen mode.

2 Tap Edit.

3 Tap the Rotate button to rotate the image if applicable.

4 Tap the Auto Enhance button to apply automatic enhancements.

5 Tap the Red-Eye button and then tap to remove red-eye in any subject (if applicable). Tap Apply.

6 Tap the Crop button and drag the rectangle to the desired part of the image.

7 Tap Crop.

8 Tap Save and then tap Save to Camera Roll.

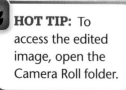 **HOT TIP:** To access the edited image, open the Camera Roll folder.

? DID YOU KNOW?

When you view a photo in full screen mode that is stored in the Camera Roll or the Photo Stream folder, a Trash button appears. You can use this to delete a photo. You will not be able to delete photos from other folders (you have to do this by syncing with your computer.)

Problem 6: I am trying to take a picture but the Camera app keeps focusing on the wrong subject

Your iPhone makes some assumptions about what you want to focus on when you frame a shot. You can tap once on the screen to tell your iPhone you want to focus on some other part of the picture. This will cause the camera to refocus and adjust the shot, and should result in a better picture.

1 Point the camera so that there are several available points of focus (perhaps a group of people standing various distances from you).

2 Wait to see what the camera focuses on. You can tell by the rectangle that appears on the screen.

3 To focus on a different part of the picture, tap the desired part.

4 Wait while the camera refocuses, then take your shot.

HOT TIP: Make sure to hold your iPhone steady and to keep your finger or thumb out of the shot!

? DID YOU KNOW?
You can delete pictures you've taken but do not want from the Photos app. Tap Camera Roll, tap the picture to delete and then tap the Trash icon.

Problem 7: I uninstalled an app and now I want it back

If you uninstall an app and decide you want it back, either:

1 Find it in the App Store and tap Install, or

2 From the App Store, tap Updates, then Purchased, and then tap the app to reinstall.

Problem 8: I purchased some media from iTunes and I want to download it to my iPhone

You may have noticed the Purchased option available from the More tab inside the iTunes app. You can tap it to view media you've purchased. You can download purchased media to your iPhone, if desired.

1 From iTunes, tap the More tab.

2 Tap Purchased.

3 Tap the desired entry.

ALERT: Movies require a lot of storage space and can quickly fill up your phone. Only download movies you'll watch soon, and delete them when you're finished.

4 Navigate to the item to download.

5 Tap the cloud icon to download the media.

Problem 9: I want to sell my iPhone. What should I do?

You can reset parts of your iPhone to factory defaults, such as the order of the apps on the Home screen, your network settings and more. You can also reset the entire phone to factory defaults. You should do this when you're ready to sell the phone or pass it on to someone else.

1 Tap Settings, General, then Reset.

2 Choose what you want to reset. If you're getting rid of the phone, choose Erase All Content and Settings.

3 If required, input your passcode lock and verify your decision.

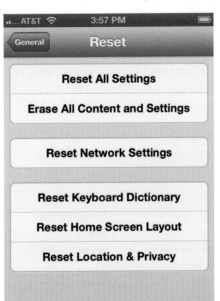

ALERT: Do not choose Erase All Content and Settings unless you are ready to sell your phone or give it away.

HOT TIP: If you want the main Home screen to look like it did when you first got it, choose to reset the Home screen layout.

Problem 10: I lost my phone and bought a replacement. How do I put my data on it?

If you've created the proper backups, you can restore a replacement phone with the data easily. It's part of the set-up process.

1 When you first turn on your new iPhone, log in with your existing Apple ID and password.

2 Know where your backups are; they are in iCloud or on your computer in iTunes.

3 When prompted, choose to populate the phone with data from a backup.

4 Choose the desired backup location. You will have to connect your iPhone to your computer to use one from iTunes.

5 If you can't restore from a backup for any reason and you have a backup in iTunes, connect your phone, right-click your iPhone in the left pane, and click Restore from Backup.

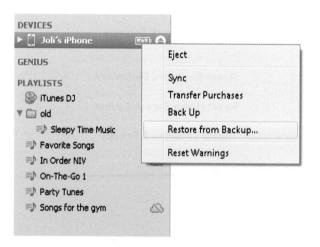

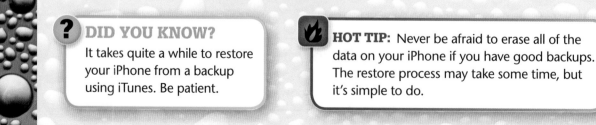

? DID YOU KNOW?
It takes quite a while to restore your iPhone from a backup using iTunes. Be patient.

🔥 HOT TIP: Never be afraid to erase all of the data on your iPhone if you have good backups. The restore process may take some time, but it's simple to do.